The Great Contest

RUSSIA AND THE WEST

The Great Contest

RUSSIA AND THE WEST

by

ISAAC DEUTSCHER

1960

OXFORD UNIVERSITY PRESS

New York and London

© *Oxford University Press 1960*

Manufactured in the United States of America

FOREWORD

In this short book I present the revised text of a series of lectures which I delivered, at the invitation of the Dafoe Foundation and the Canadian Institute of International Affairs, in Montreal, Toronto, and Winnipeg last autumn. I am publishing this book at the request of the sponsors of the lectures, supported by many requests from my audiences, and in the belief that what is said here about the Soviet Union and the state of international affairs may be of interest to wider circles of readers.

This survey begins with a brief summary of recent Soviet domestic developments. I have here tried to bring up-to-date the analysis of social and political trends which I first formulated in 1953, immediately after Stalin's death, when in my book *Russia After Stalin*[1] I made an emphatic forecast of de-Stalinization. I am including, as a pendant, a lecture on 'The Moral and Intellectual Climate of the Soviet Union', given at the Annual Conference of the Alumni Association of the University of Manitoba. The Conference discussed 'The Place of the University in Modern Society'; and it is with special reference to that topic that I have dealt with Soviet intellectual life.

My review of the domestic scene is, however, given only by way of introduction to my main theme, which is Soviet foreign policy and the state of international affairs. The need for such an introduction is due to the fact that the foreign policy of any government, especially of the Soviet Government, is a prolongation of its domestic policy. This is all too often forgotten in a period of 'summit' meetings, when the public is led to believe that three or four Big Men solve, or fail to solve, the world's predicaments according to whether they have or do not have the wisdom, the good will, or the magic wand needed for their task. I have endeavoured to concentrate attention on the

[1] In the United States the book was published under the title *Russia: What Next?* in June 1953.

v

essential motives and the long-term aspirations of Soviet policy
and to probe the 'stalemate of fears' that characterizes the
present state of world diplomacy.

Finally, in the last chapter I attempt to bring into the open
those implications of 'peaceful coexistence and competition'
which are still largely hidden but which, in my view, will
determine the outcome of the Great Contest between East and
West in the last quarter of this century, if not earlier. I do not
expect my argument to be widely accepted; but it will serve its
purpose if it turns attention to the less obvious aspects of the
problem under discussion. In conclusion I am making—
without, I trust, either simplification or sentimentality—a plea
for disarmament.

I would like to express gratitude to the sponsors of my Dafoe
Foundation lectures, Mr. Victor Sifton, Chairman of the
Foundation, and Mr. George V. Ferguson, Chairman of the
Canadian Institute of International Affairs, and also to the
Nuffield Foundation. My thanks are also due to many friends
in Canada and to the large audiences whose friendly attention
and intelligent and alert interest in international affairs have
greatly stimulated my own thinking on these matters.

I. D.

30 March, 1960

CONTENTS

The Great Contest

RUSSIA AND THE WEST

I

THE KHRUSHCHEV INTERREGNUM

THE few years that have passed since Stalin's death must be counted a very short period in history. Yet in the life of the Soviet Union these have been crucial years, crowded with events behind which one could sense a 'change in climate', the work of many socio-political impulses, and the gathering of a fresh historic momentum in the fortunes of a great state and nation. At times abruptly and dramatically, and at other times slowly and almost imperceptibly, the Soviet Union has moved away from Stalinism. How far has it gone? And where is it going?

It is no longer possible to doubt that since 1953 the Soviet Union has been in the throes of a deep revulsion against Stalinism. So strong, so overwhelming indeed, has been this revulsion that no open attempt to preserve the Stalinist system of government as a whole has been made or could be made with any chance of success. Yet the revulsion does not amount to any wholesale rejection of the record of the Stalin era. It could not amount to that. The evaluation of that record will probably remain a matter of historical and political controversy for a long time; but already it is clear that this has been a record of extraordinary complexity, compounded of huge assets and huge liabilities which it is not easy to disentangle.

The Soviet Union emerged from the Stalin era in a condition very different from that in which it had entered it; and both rulers and ruled alike have been deeply conscious of the difference. Having been one of the world's most backward and poverty-stricken nations, in many respects closer to India and China than to the West, the Soviet Union has risen, within the lifetime of a single generation, to the rank of the world's second industrial power. In the 1920s many of its peasants still tilled the land with wooden ploughs; in the 1950s the Soviet Union played the leading part in developing nuclear technology. At the outset of the Stalin era only about one-tenth of the Soviet manpower was employed in modern industry; at present nearly one half of it is so employed. In thirty years the urban population of the U.S.S.R. has grown by about 75 million people. The old cities and towns have greatly expanded and many new ones have sprung into being. Where there had been illiteracy and a primordially primitive way of life, an extensive network of schools was built up; and now the Soviet people are probably the world's most educated nation possessed of an unquenchable thirst for more education.

The debit side of the balance is quite as stupendous: Russia's rise to the rank of the world's second industrial power had not been accompanied by any comparable rise in popular standards of living; these were abysmally low at the close of the Stalin era. The development of the Soviet planned economy had been lopsided: the needs and interests of the mass of consumers had been utterly disregarded. Apart from the general scarcity of goods, the shortage of housing and the urban overcrowding had become a national calamity. The nation was overflowing with political discontents. The workers, oppressed by a draconic labour code, an inhuman factory discipline, and the fear of the slave labour camp, were at the mercy of managers and party bosses; they could seek no redress through the trade unions. And they resented the inequalities fostered by Stalin's economic and social policies which favoured the bureaucrats and split the working class into a well paid and privileged minority and an underpaid majority.

The peasants chafed at the bureaucratic tutelage under which they lived and worked. They were not allowed to till the collective farms as they pleased; and the government's requisition squads wrested from them half the crops. The peasants' sullen discontent was responsible for the stagnant condition of farming, which prevented any adequate improvement of the urban standard of living.

Finally, the intelligentsia suffered from the stranglehold of the official orthodoxy from which they could not escape—the orthodox censor ruled supreme in every field of science, literature, and art. Riddled with spies and informers, all social classes hated the police state; and all were becoming more or less disgusted with the grotesque Stalin cult.

Rarely in history has the record of any epoch consisted of so many and of such striking contrasts; and rarely, if ever, did any nation view any chapter of its history with such mixed and intense feelings, with so much pride and so much shame. As I have said, the difficulty consisted—and still consists—in disentangling the various elements of the Stalinist legacy—the good and the evil had often been inextricably intertwined. This has accounted for much of the ambiguity of the Soviet attitude towards the Stalin era, an ambiguity which I shall have to discuss repeatedly in the course of these lectures. Yet through all this ambiguity the urge for change and reform broke irresistibly.

The pressure for de-Stalinization was irresistible even in 1953–56, before the Twentieth Congress of the Communist Party, but it also was—and still is—politically inarticulate. It was irresistible because of its universal character: all social classes felt that they could not go on living as before. It was inarticulate because no class and no group could express itself politically, or formulate a programme of reform, and fight for its realization. Decades of totalitarian rule had left the nation politically atomized. Yet the reaction against Stalinism had been prepared by the nation's industrial and cultural growth that had taken place in these same decades. The Stalinist autocracy, discipline, and orthodoxy had been rooted in the soil and in the primitive traditions of pre-industrial Russia or had been grafted on to them. Stalin exploited and over-exploited these traditions in order to discipline the nation throughout the period of forced industrialization and collectivization. But, after the great industrial advance had been achieved, that discipline lost its relative justification and its effectiveness; and the traditions which had sustained it for so long were losing their grip.

A predominantly rural and illiterate Russia could prostrate herself in awe before a twentieth-century reincarnation of Ivan the Terrible. An urbanized and educated people grew sick of the prostration. Uprooted barefoot *muzhiks*, driven by the millions into newly-built factories and bewildered by the unfamiliar rhythm of industrial life, submitted or were made to submit to a labour code which had been designed to break them forcibly to the habits of industrial work. An advanced, increasingly stable, skilled, and educated working class felt insulted by the indignities of such a labour code. The hectic competition of workers at the factory bench—the competition for higher output and higher pay rates known as Stakhanovism—may have stimulated up to a point the efficiency of the muzhiks-turned-workers; but with industrial progress Stakhanovism was becoming economically wasteful as was also the extreme anti-egalitarianism of Stalin's labour policy. The simmering social antagonisms produced by that policy might have reached explosion point if nothing had been done to mitigate them.

It was easy to see with what demands workers and peasants would have come forward if they had been politically vocal. The workers surely would have clamoured for the abolition of the Stalinist labour code, for a new relationship between management and labour; for a revival of trade unions and of their freedom to defend the workers' interests; for a new wages policy which would reduce the extreme discrepancies between high and low earnings; for a modification of economic policy and a greatly increased output of consumer goods; for adequate housing; and finally, for a degree of workers' control over industry.

Such a minimum programme of reform would have been based on the workers' daily experience and needs; being mainly economic in character, it would still have left untouched the great issues of national and international policy. We know now from many reports, independent and official, that the workers did indeed exercise pressure in favour of such demands; the pressure was unorganized, fitful, and local in scale: it showed itself only within the factory or the workshop. It did not

5

grow wider and assume any recognizable form of a national movement. It was not only that Stalin's successors were bent on suppressing any spontaneous and autonomous working-class activity. The impulse for such activity appears to have been rather feeble. Having lived for decades under totalitarian rule, the present generation of Soviet workers has had no significant experience of self-expression and self-organization. They have never had the opportunity to form their own independent organizations, groups, or even discussion circles, to formulate demands, to support these by industrial action, to elect their true representatives, and so on. They could not learn to do all these things overnight, especially when those in power were indeed doing their utmost to prevent them from learning. Thus the discontent of the working class remained politically mute.

If such was the condition of the industrial workers, who were numerically already the strongest class in the Soviet Union, the state of mind of the rural population could not be different. In every respect the peasantry is no longer what it used to be. It has shrunk and has become a minority of the nation. It suffered a terrible holocaust in the last war: most of the 20 million people who lost their lives in the war had been peasants; for a long time after the war only women, old men, cripples, and children could be seen tilling the fields in Russia and the Ukraine. It can be imagined how this catastrophe affected the spirit of rural Russia. The peasantry had never had much capacity for political self-expression and organization; now it had less of it than ever.

Yet the peasants did find some outlets for their resentment. Only reluctantly and sluggishly did they till the land; they produced little and kept the nation on short and insecure rations; they compelled the government to fight grim 'battles of bread' year-in-year-out; and they imperilled thereby the prospects of industrialization. The peasantry's demands, even if they remained unformulated, were clear enough, for they were inherent in the situation. In all probability the great majority of the peasants no longer hankered after private farming. A new generation of *Kolkhozniki* had grown up who knew little or nothing of it. In the course of a quarter of a century the collective structure of agriculture had to some extent become consolidated. After a massive mechanization of farming, conceived in a manner suitable only for large-scale farms, there could be no question of any restoration of the old smallholding. Any attempt at this could result only in a total disruption of agriculture and in nation-wide famine. But within the framework of the collective farm the peasantry pressed for greater freedom of initiative, for its right to benefit from the fruits of its labour, for an end to the ruthless requisitioning of farm produce, for a more abundant supply of industrial goods, and for more advantageous terms in the economic exchange between town and country. Unuttered, the peasantry's demands could be heard by all.

The situation of the intelligentsia, the professional classes, and the bureaucracy was in many respects different from that of the workers and peasants. These were the privileged groups of the Stalin era, who had benefited from Stalin's anti-egalitarian policies. He had allowed them and aided them to grab abundant slices of the national loaf while the rest of the nation starved. Yet it was from them that the cry 'Not by bread alone . . .'

presently came. Men of letters, artists, and scientists, all those whose job it was to produce ideas or artistic images, revolted against the ubiquitous orthodoxy which exercised an obtuse censorship over ideas and images. They refused to be ideological robots. Physicists and agronomists in particular, protested against the incompetent supervision of their work, even at the laboratory, by party hacks, a supervision which impeded the progress of the entire national economy.

The writers became for a time the spearhead of the reform movement, not because they were exceptionally brave—men like Ehrenburg had been among Stalin's most servile sycophants. But in a mute nation the writers were the only group capable of self-expression. Even after decades of censorship and writing to order, they still retained that capacity, however crippled. And so, men who had for so long been Stalin's intellectual slaves, suddenly became the mouth-pieces of a nation in silent revolt. In any nation leading even a half-way healthy political life, mediocre novels like Ehrenburg's *Thaw* and Dudintsev's *Not by Bread Alone* . . . could never have had the effect they had in Russia where the very titles sounded like clarion calls. Millions of people identified themselves with Ehrenburg's and Dudintsev's heroes who recorded the miseries and indignities to which they had been exposed.

A further and even more significant paradox was that large sections of the bureaucracy itself were drawn into the protest against bureaucratic despotism. It was the men of the party machine, the administrators, and the industrial managers, who had raised Stalin to the pinnacle of power and had been his props. But once at the pinnacle, the autocrat kicked down his own props.

Even among his closest supporters and associates none was safe. And so when he died the whole of the nation could hear the subdued sigh of relief from the supposedly all-powerful Presidium; and the sigh was echoed at all levels of the tremendous bureaucratic pyramid. Of course, the privileged bureaucracy, too, had their grievances and their hopes. The industrial managers hoped to rid themselves of the over-centralized control which deprived them of the initiative and the freedom of action essential to efficient management. Administrators and party bosses, from Moscow down to the remotest corners of the country, were relieved to think that this was the end of the autocrat's whimsical and tyrannical meddling with their affairs. Thus almost all the echelons of the bureaucracy were at one with the intelligentsia and the people at large in the reaction against Stalinism. This was a fact of decisive importance, for if in a nation reduced to political passivity and silence, the intelligentsia alone could speak up, it was the bureaucracy alone that could act.

These then were the facts that determined the subsequent evolution of the Soviet Union: the universal revulsion against Stalinism, and the momentary concord in this mood between rulers and ruled; the inevitability of reform, which would remove the Stalinist brakes on national efficiency; the inability of the basic social classes, the workers and the peasants, to assert themselves, and the absence of any articulate and organized political movement from below; and, finally, the awareness within the ruling group itself of the need for reform and its relative willingness to meet that need. In the absence of any significant anti-Stalinist movement from below reform could come only from above, from the Stalinist ruling group. Yet when the decisive agent in reforming a bureaucratic system is the bureaucracy itself, the reform must be self-contradictory and limited. Its aim is to rationalize the method of government, not to subject the government to social and political control from below. After a rule as irrational and full of excesses as Stalin's, the mere rationalization of the method of government and the abandonment of 'excesses' constitute by themselves important progress. Shortly after Stalin's death, I compared this situation with that which prevailed in Russia after the death of Tsar Nicolas I, in 1855, when all that was progressive in Russia yearned for the abolition of serfdom, but, as there was no significant movement from below capable of achieving it, Tsar Alexander II became the 'emancipator' of the peasants. I predicted that something similar would happen presently: the Stalinist ruling group itself would be compelled to 'liberalize' the method of government and to break the backbone of the police-state, which, with its slave-labour camps and terror, had been the contemporary equivalent of serfdom. But Tsar Alexander II could not abolish serfdom consistently, in a manner satisfactory to the peasantry. Nor could Stalin's successors carry out de-Stalinization consistently, in a manner designed to meet fully the nation's needs. They had all been Stalin's willing or unwilling accomplices. They all had a stake in Stalinism. They could not afford to expose fully all the festering sores of the Stalin era. Khrushchev and Malenkov, not to speak of Molotov, Beria, Kaganovich, and others, who had helped Stalin to stage his bloody purges, to set up his concentration camps, to exterminate all his opponents, could not tell the full truth about all this. Yet the full truth had—and still has—to be told before the evils could be eradicated truly and once for all. Without such a whole-hearted exposure it was—and still is—impossible to overcome Stalinism totally and to transcend it.

It may be asked why has a great nation, in a moment of an overwhelming urge for self-purification, not been able to bring forward men with untainted records, men other than Stalin's epigones? The answer is in all its grimness very simple: all the leaders of anti-Stalinist opinion had been exterminated, and a nation for so long politically atomized could not produce new leaders overnight. De-Stalinization had become a national necessity for the Soviet Union, but as there were no anti-Stalinists to carry it out, the job fell of necessity to the leading Stalinists who could do no more than half the job. The task was imposed on them by circumstances, but it remained uncongenial to them. They faced it divided among themselves, and divided in their own minds, torn between frankness and hypocrisy, between courage and fear, between their stake in Stalinism and their desire to break away from Stalinism, between the past and the future.

The struggles and the rivalries among Stalin's successors have reflected these dilemmas. The divisions between reformers and conservatives, de-Stalinizers and Stalinist die-hards have manifested themselves over every major issue of policy. The manner in which the struggle has been conducted has also reflected the contradictions of the situation. The ruling group has been both clinging to its Stalinist habits and shedding them. In no one can this conflict be seen more clearly than in Khrushchev himself. In his struggle for power he has behaved like Stalin and yet quite unlike Stalin. He, too, has held a centre position between the opposed groups and has appropriated the ideas now of one set of his opponents and now of another. He has done more than anyone else to explode the Stalinist orthodoxy, but he has also been its defender. He has eliminated his opponents and rivals right and left; but, apart from the special case of Beria, he has not so far proceeded to exterminate them—he has not even expelled Malenkov or Molotov from the party. He appears to have done away with collective leadership, as Stalin did; yet he has not become the autocrat that Stalin was. He holds fast to the principle of the monolithic party, in which no dissent from the official view, that is from his view, must be voiced. Yet he does not denounce the dissenter as the enemy of the people; he even warns zealots against ideological witch-hunts. He embodies the revulsion against Stalinism and the attachment to Stalinism alike.

Considering the character and the political traditions of the ruling group and of Khrushchev himself, the surprising thing is not that they have carried out reform only half-heartedly and that they have tried to salvage what they can of the Stalinist system, but that they have salvaged so little of it, and that they have carried out so many and such important reforms. More than once indeed have they tried to reverse de-Stalinization. They did so first after the 1953 Berlin rising, and then at the time of the civil war in Hungary, to mention only these two critical turns. Both these events brought home to them the dangers and risks inherent in de-Stalinization and temporarily strengthened the hands of the opponents of reform. (It was no matter of chance that a few months after the fighting in Budapest, Molotov and Kaganovich were almost on the point of overthrowing Khrushchev.)

Yet so far every attempt to stem the tide of reform has had only limited and short-lived success. Stemmed in one sector of public life, it breaks through in another and there spreads irresistibly. By riding that tide Khrushchev has risen to the top and maintained himself there. However much he may have done to defend the Stalinist orthodoxy, to the Soviet people he remains the hero of de-Stalinization, the celebrated author of the 'secret speech' at the Twentieth Congress. He himself has been aware of this and has done his best to capitalize his reputation as reformer. His deadliest weapon against his rivals has been the charge that they are conservatives bent on prolonging the evils of the Stalin era—evidently nothing can bring as much popular discredit upon a political leader in the Soviet Union today as does this accusation. Stalinism has been able to fight only rear-guard battles. Its retreat continues.

The long series of recent reforms has aimed at raising economic and social efficiency and also at meeting half way the unformulated desiderata of the various social classes and groups. I have said that the political police have been tamed and that society has been freed from the intense terror under which it had lived. This process, which had begun well before Khrushchev's rise but has continued since, found its formal expression in the principles of the new criminal code designed, to quote the official preamble, 'to liquidate the shameful heritage of the past'. The political police are deprived of the power to sentence, imprison, and deport Soviet citizens; and the secret trial, guilt by association, collective res-ponsibility, and many other ill-famed features of Stalin-ist 'justice' are being abolished. By itself the promul-gation of new laws offers, of course, no guarantee of any genuine rule of law and one must still treat with reserve Khrushchev's claim that not a single political offender is imprisoned in the Soviet Union today. However, the change from the Stalin era is unmistakable; and many independent and critical Western visitors have borne witness to it.

Next in importance among the reforms is the curtailment of the powers of the bureaucracy at large. Here the most striking act has been the disbandment of the numerous economic ministries which used to exercise from Moscow a rigid and minute control over the whole of the national economy. Clearly, this type of over-centralized control had to be swept away for the sake of efficiency. Over a hundred regional Economic Councils have taken the place of the ministries. No doubt, within these Councils the provincial bureaucratic element remains strongly entrenched. But as the reform has been carried out with the cry for a revival of local initiative, the provincial bureaucracy cannot monopolize the benefits. Within the regional Councils a new balance between manager and worker has been forming: the workers are no longer at the mercy of the managers. The prerogatives of the trade unions have been enlarged; the unions have been reminded of their duty to defend the workers' interests; and the role of the factory councils has grown. The abatement of the police terror, and the promises of new labour codes and of a new criminal code have changed the atmosphere in industry too. The worker is no longer haunted by the fear of the slave-labour camp; he cannot be punished for minor industrial offences or branded as an enemy of the people when he tries to speak up for himself.

Renascent working-class egalitarianism dictates further changes in labour policy. The government has had to do away at least with the excesses of the Stalinist anti-egalitarianism. It has recast the structure of wages, narrowed the gap between high and low incomes, raised the salaries and pensions of the underpaid and put a ceiling on some high incomes and pensions. This policy is backed up by continuous efforts to increase the output of consumer goods faster than had been planned and to mitigate the appalling housing conditions. This new deal for the working class culminates in the introduction of the 40-hour week in industry and the promise of a further shortening of the working week to 30–35 hours within the coming decade.

The farmers too have had a 'new deal', of which up to a few years ago they could only dream. For the first time in forty years compulsory deliveries of food have been abolished—that compulsion had been the scourge of the peasantry. This is not to say that farmers are free to market their goods as they do in any capitalist country. The state is the chief purchaser of agricultural produce and as such it enjoys quasi-monopolistic advantages. But in its relations with the farmers the state is now content to rely on its economic preponderance rather than on coercion. The government is anxious to give the peasantry a stake in the general national development and to shake it out of that condition of resentfulness and alienation from urban Russia in which Stalinist policy had kept it. The farmer is no longer told what he should grow, and how and when he should grow it. The government has raised considerably the prices it pays for agricultural produce. More startlingly, it has wound up the state-owned Machine Tractor Stations through which it had controlled the rural economy;

and it has sold the machines and tractors to the collective farms. It should be recalled that shortly before Stalin's death the Machine Tractor Stations were at the centre of an important debate, and Stalin decided in favour of their continued state ownership on the ground that the sale of tractors and machines to the peasantry would weaken the socialist character of the economy. Khrushchev has nevertheless ventured to carry out this reform in the belief that state-owned industry, with its greatly expanded resources and power, has nothing to fear from an increase in the economic strength of farming. In any case, the government offers the farmers *individual* incentives in order to strengthen the *collective* framework of agriculture.

Side by side with these reforms, intensive amalgamation and concentration of collective farms goes on. The whole pattern of farming is changing and becoming determined by a highly modern technology, specialization, and nation-wide division of labour. This is indeed an extraordinary transformation: thirty years ago there were still some 25 million primitive smallholdings in the country; last year there were only 70 or 80 thousand collective farms; and by 1965 there should be left only ten thousand fully electrified collective farms (apart from the Sovkhozy, the state-owned farms). The last few years have brought a steep rise in agricultural productivity, but it may still be too early to say whether or at what pace the rise will continue.

Surveying the Soviet scene, one is struck by the contrast between the bold sweep of economic and social reforms and the timid conservatism and stagnation in the strictly political field. The contrast has been particularly sharp since the civil war in Hungary, which came as a shock and in the political field brought de-Stalinization to a halt. The effects of that shock have not yet been lived down. After his iconoclastic outburst at the Twentieth Congress, Khrushchev appears to have been busy putting the icons back into the old places. He, the arch-revisionist of 1956, has launched the campaign against 'revisionism'. Under this convenient label are lumped together the disillusioned ex-Stalinists who have come to doubt and abandon the basic tenets of communism, and those who have been pressing for further reforms and de-Stalinization within the framework of communism. The former have represented an important, and at times the prevalent, current of opinion in Hungary, Poland, and other Eastern European countries, but not, it seems, within the Soviet Union, where the call for de-Stalinization and reform has drawn inspiration from the pre-Stalinist Bolshevik tradition, from Leninism. To that tradition belongs the '*democratic* centralism' which is being opposed to the 'bureaucratic centralism' of the Stalin era and which implies free and open debate, at least within the party and the trade unions, over major issues of policy and organization; and the freedom of the rank and file to choose between conflicting viewpoints and to elect their leaders. In none of these respects, however, has Khrushchevism moved far away from Stalinism, and where it has moved away it has been retracing its steps. No genuinely free and public debate has yet taken place over any major issue of policy—even Khrushchev's Twentieth Congress speech still remains 'secret'. No open clash of views is permitted; even where such a clash is known to have developed, as in the conflict between Khrushchev and Molotov and Malenkov, the party's monolithic façade and the pretence of absolute unanimity have been kept up.

The official propaganda departments have worked to re-establish their control over literature and art, and, to a much lesser extent, even over science. A halt has been called in paι ιcular to all attempts to probe into the truth about the Stalin era, and even that part of it which was revealed in 1956 is being hushed up. It is as if Khrushchev, having revealed the skeleton in the Stalinist cupboard, were now trying to slam the door on it and pretend that nothing had happened.

This ambiguity of Khrushchevism puts a question mark over some of the reforms and over much of the progress achieved. It spreads uncertainty, doubt, even fear among Soviet people. They do not know, after all, which is real: Khrushchev's repudiation of Stalinist oppression or his repudiation of the repudiation. As long as Stalin's misdeeds are officially both condemned and excused, there is no certainty that Stalin's successors will not make themselves guilty of similar misdeeds. The arbitrary rule of the political police has disappeared; but may it not come back? The government has in economic and social matters ceased to rely on brute coercion, but will it not resort to it once again? The bureaucrats have yielded ground to workers and peasants and given up some privileges. But have they yielded that ground for good, and are they not going to recapture it? Uncertainty damps the 'initiative of the masses', on which so many hopes are placed and which is indeed essential to national efficiency and sanity.

This ambiguity weighs most heavily on the intelligentsia, those mouthpieces of the mute nation. Khrushchev has all too obviously been anxious to discipline them and to curb their reformist fervour. Writers, artists, and ideologues who have shown too strong a propensity to independent thinking have been reminded of the still prevailing rigours of orthodoxy. Historians have been warned not to delve into the mysteries of the recent past and not to take it for granted that they are altogether free from the duty to falsify history. They should not indeed forget the skeleton in the cupboard that Khrushchev has shown them; but they must not remember it too well either. They are required to possess a good historical memory when needed, and, when this becomes embarrassing, to exhibit complete amnesia. The same or similar ambiguities can be found in many other fields, and one can well imagine the agony of an intelligentsia who have perpetually to adjust themselves to such contradictory demands.

Yet even in their attempts to resuscitate the old controls and discipline Khrushchev and his supporters have been half-hearted. No sooner do they try to subject the intelligentsia to arbitrary dictates than they are compelled to demonstrate that they did not mean to impose any such dictates. No sooner do they damn a heresy than they feel the need to excuse themselves and to show that they are not engaging in any Stalinist witch-hunt. Thus, almost every attempt at the re-enforcement of orthodoxy is followed by the plea for tolerance towards the unorthodox; and every act of re-Stalinization is veiled or softened or undone by the reminder that de-Stalinization is on.

All these contradictions make of the present state of affairs something transient and provisional. Despite his great self-confidence, untameable vigour, and slapdash drive, Khrushchev presides over what can be only a relatively unstable and short interregnum. What lies ahead is not a Khrushchev era comparable to the Stalin era. Not only are Khrushchev's days as grass—he has risen to power in his sixties, whereas Stalin did so in his forties. Far more important is the tremendous flux in which Soviet society finds itself, and by which it is being transformed so rapidly that the passage of only a few years renders obsolete and makes untenable relations, institutions, laws, and political practices which have long seemed to be deep-rooted and almost indestructible. This flux has broken through the heavy crust of Stalinism; it will break through the much thinner and flimsier crust of Khrushchevism.

The Soviet Union of the 1960s will be even more different from the Soviet Union of the 1950s than this has been from the Soviet Union of the 1940s and 1930s. Ahead are new and immense strides in industrialization, modernization, technology, science, and mass education which arc all going to bring about changes in the moral and political climate, changes deeper than those we have witnessed so far. Despite all the progress achieved hitherto, there still exist vast areas of backwardness and primitivism in the Soviet Union today; and it is the strength of Khrushchevism that it is the authentic product of this mixture of progress and backwardness. There is still much of the old muzhik in Khrushchev himself—he is the muzhik who has reached the threshold of the atomic age, the last muzhik to speak in the name of Russia and to represent her on the world stage.

In another few years there will be hardly a trace left of the Russia of the muzhiks. A new working class is growing up. Already in the 1950s most of the young workers who came to the factory bench had received secondary education. They have played their part in changing the atmosphere in industry. They have behaved towards managers and party bosses with the self-assurance that comes with education. With every year the weight of these educated 'factory hands' is growing; and demands for workers' control of industry will acquire new meaning with the workers' growing ability to exercise such control. There is undoubtedly an important core of truth in Soviet claims that the Soviet method of mass education is narrowing the gulf between manual labour and brain work. It was in the abysmal depth of that gulf that the Russian bureaucratic absolutism—and Stalinism—had been rooted; and one can foresee that the narrowing and bridging of the gulf will render obsolete and impossible even the milder, the Khrushchevite form of bureaucratic dictatorship.

The dynamics of economic and cultural growth determine the prospects of domestic policy. The Soviet Union is an expanding society, emerging from a period of 'primitive socialist accumulation', rapidly increasing its wealth, and enabling all classes and groups to enlarge their shares of the national income. This makes for a relaxation of social tensions and antagonisms. On the other hand, the social and cultural advance tends to make the masses aware of the fact that they are deprived of political liberties and are ruled by an uncontrolled bureaucracy. In coming years this will impel them to seek freedom of expression and association, even if this should bring them into conflict with the ruling bureaucracy. No one can foresee with certainty whether the conflict will take violent and explosive forms and lead to the new 'political revolution' which Trotsky once advocated, or whether the conflict will be resolved peacefully through bargaining, compromise, and the gradual enlargement of freedom. Much will depend on the behaviour of those in power, on their sensitivity and readiness to yield in time to popular pressures. Towards the end of the Stalin era the antagonisms and tensions within Soviet society were acute; and if the ruling group had rigidly clung to the Stalinist method of government, it might have provoked a political explosion. This did not happen, however; and in consequence of the reforms carried out since 1953 the social and political tensions have been greatly reduced. Should the ruling group attempt to cancel these reforms, then it would certainly heighten the tensions once again and exacerbate the antagonisms. But if the government remains flexible and sensitive to popular demands, there will be little likelihood of any explosive internal development. The prospect would then be one of further gradual reform, of increasing well-being and social contentment, and of growing freedom.

At present the evidence points towards a strong current of high hope running through all sections of Soviet society, towards the sense of exhilaration that a vital and expanding society gives its members, and the sense of moral solidarity that comes from the consciousness of a high purpose animating the body politic. There is also a strong and widespread awareness of how much remains to be done, how great are the inadequacies of the present Soviet way of life, and how much liberty has still to be gained.

This state of mind is aptly illustrated in an account of a journey to the Soviet Union given by a Russian-born traveller from the West. Speaking to his former compatriots, the traveller finds that they all believe that the

Soviet Union is destined to become not only the most efficient and the wealthiest but also 'the freest country in the world—*at least* as free as any country in the West'. On this all seem to be agreed. Their differences begin when they are asked how much time it will take before they attain the freedom for which they hope. The optimists say: three years; the pessimists reply: at least thirty.

I am inclined to think that a realistic prospect may well lie somewhere between the two extremes.

II

THE MORAL AND INTELLECTUAL CLIMATE*

THE Soviet Union has been in a state of great intellectual and moral ferment these last years, and the university and the educational system at large have, naturally enough, been drawn into it. One could sense this *inter alia* in the debate on education and on the reform of the school system which recently took place all over the Soviet Union.

The debate and the reform have reflected the peculiar dilemmas and difficulties with which Soviet education has to contend. Let me say at once that these are dilemmas and difficulties which bring credit to the Soviet Union. The essence of the problem lies in the fact that the extraordinary expansion of Soviet education has in some respects outrun the nation's economic resources. To us this may seem a paradoxical development, because here, in the West, we see the opposite phenomenon: our educational systems are sadly and scandalously underdeveloped in relation to our wealth. And yet this is the fact: the Russians have expanded their schools almost beyond their means. What an enviable mistake!

Shortly after Stalin's death the Soviet government abolished all school fees and declared education of all

---

* This lecture was given at the Annual Conference of the Alumni Association of the University of Manitoba held in October 1959.

grades to be free for all. In recent years secondary education has become universal in the cities and towns, where half the population is now living; and it has been rapidly spreading over the rural parts of the Soviet Union as well. As a result of this, every year in the late 1950s many hundreds of thousands of graduates of secondary schools knocked at university gates, but could not be accepted. There was an overall shortage of facilities. Naturally enough, the government could not open new universities and colleges as rapidly as it had been opening new secondary schools. The Soviet Union has now forty leading state universities compared with only ten in the whole Tsarist Empire (or fourteen, if the universities in pre-1914 Poland and Finland are included). The present Seven Year Plan provides for a remarkable extension of academic facilities: there should be four and a half million university graduates in 1965 compared with only three million at present. All the same, the expansion of academic facilities has failed to keep pace with the growth of secondary education.

This was the difficulty with which the latest Education Act, passed in December 1958, had to contend. In effect Khrushchev had to fight a battle at the university gates in order to drive the overflow of would-be students from lecture halls to factory benches. Apart from the circumstance that the universities could not absorb all the candidates, there was the danger that industry might run short of manpower, especially as these were the years when the war-time fall in the birthrate began to show in the balance of industrial manpower. Someone has to produce the goods on which the nation's livelihood depends. (Incidentally, in driving masses of would-be students to the factories, Khrushchev may have been

storing up trouble for himself and his bureaucracy—
these young and educated workers will be anything but
clay in the hands of party bosses and industrial managers.)

The debate over the Education Act was instructive.
Khrushchev had intended to curtail secondary education
quite drastically, to lower the school leaving age, to
channel pupils into several 'streams' (as they are
channelled in English schools), so as to reduce at the
source, at the secondary school, the number of candidates for academic training. However, many of these
proposals provoked widespread if cautiously worded
protests from parents and teachers alike—even children
protested; and so Khrushchev thought it wise to modify
his original draft and to propose a compromise. This was
accepted on the understanding that it was provisional;
and the government had to commit itself at once to a
further expansion of the universities and it increased
the budgetary grants for all grades of schools.

The Soviet people have thus shown that they are in
no mood to allow their rulers to cheat their appetite, or
rather craving, for education. What deserves special
attention is the provision for extra-mural education.
Because academic facilities were short and industry
wanted manpower, extra-mural academic education
(which forms only one sector of a ramified system of
adult education) has acquired exceptional importance.
The number of extra-mural worker-students preparing
for academic degrees is about half the number of full
time undergraduates. (In history, for instance, 17,500
factory workers are studying for academic degrees.)
The government pays much of the cost of this education.
According to a decree of 2 July 1959, the extra-mural
worker-student gets four to six weeks fully paid leave

every year from his factory to enable him to prepare for annual examinations; in his final year he gets a day off every week and a study holiday of one or two months, with a stipend, but no wages. The government pays the travelling expenses the extra-mural student incurs in connexion with examinations.

This is an important development, characteristic, I believe, of the moral and intellectual climate. Mr. Adlai Stevenson, speaking from observation, has remarked recently that education and the reading of serious literature are 'a universal pastime' in the Soviet Union. It seems to me that they are a universal passion rather than a pastime. The classics of Russian and world literature are sold in millions, even tens of millions, of copies. This is perhaps not surprising, since the Soviet public is not exposed to the commercialized sensationalism rampant in the West. Gutter literature and gutter entertainment being barred, and current fiction having relatively few attractions to offer, the broad public has no choice but to read the old masterpieces.

I have said that one of the motives behind the Education Act was the government's determination to drive aspiring young men from the university to the factory. To justify this Khrushchev has talked a great deal about the need to combine manual labour with brain work. The aspiration, however, to combine these two kinds of work has deeper motives as well. It shows itself not only in the encouragement given to extra-mural education. The combination of manual labour and brain work is the corner-stone of the doctrine of polytechnical education. This is not a new doctrine. It was expounded by Karl Marx who borrowed it from French Utopian socialists; it had ardent advocates among North Ameri-

27

can educationists—John Dewey's ideas were very akin to it. In Russia experiments in polytechnical education were started in the early years of the revolution, but were then abandoned partly because the polytechnical school requires as background a far more industrialized environment than the Soviet environment of the 1920s, and partly because the experiment accorded ill with the authoritarian spirit of Stalin's educational policy.

In recent years polytechnical education has been coming back into its own. Its aim is to produce a balanced human personality, to combine development of intellectual capacity with that of physical efficiency and industrial skill, and thus to overcome the age-old divorce between intellectual work and manual–productive labour. This aspiration is beginning to permeate the schools. The curricula are designed so as to combine theory and practice and to make sure that the student grows up not in an artificially isolated 'academic world' but with first-hand experience of life and work in factory and on farm and with a sense of social affairs far richer and wider than he could obtain hitherto.

It is often said that the Soviet educational system is designed mainly to foster technology and science and that it does this in a spirit of narrow utilitarianism. There is truth in this. Obviously, in a nation industrializing at so extraordinarily rapid a pace an exaggerated emphasis on technology and science must be expected. In fact, this emphasis is far more one-sided than it need have been. Classical studies have been almost completely abandoned. This may be explained in part as a reaction against the pre-revolutionary over-emphasis on classical scholarship. Whatever the reasons, the result is a certain impoverishment of the intellectual background of the new Soviet generation. (Karl Marx would not have been what he was if he had not been steeped in classical literature—in his mature age he used to re-read in the original the whole of Euripides almost every year.) But it would be wrong to suggest that the humanities are altogether neglected. Something is being done to strike a balance between them and science. To take once again an illustration from history: there are in the Soviet Union 154 academic history departments, with 1,400 teachers. It is officially admitted that the quality of the teaching leaves much to be desired: too many teachers had to be too hastily trained. This, however, is a defect natural in the circumstances and likely to be remedied in time. The teaching of modern languages and literature is superb. The school does, on the whole, seek to forestall the worst effects of the departmentalization and fragmentation of modern knowledge. It seeks to avoid the narrowness of outlook that goes with growing specialization. We can think very critically of the dogmatic character of Soviet education—I certainly do. We can dislike all the trickery of official indoctrination—I certainly do. But there is also a positive and rational aspect to that indoctrination. It is this: the Soviet school rightly insists on the need for the specializing student to form a philosophical view of the world and not to become encrusted in his own speciality. This is a sound principle in itself. A school inspired by it may produce not just technicians who know more and more about less and less, but people combining detailed empirical knowledge with a broad view of life.

In some respects Soviet education is extremely dogmatic and indeed sterile; but in others its methods are bold and inventive. Sometimes it is the sterility that strikes the eye; sometimes it is the fertility of ideas. You may ask: what is the balance? The answer cannot perhaps be as clear-cut as I should like. Soviet intellectual life (especially in the universities) still feels the heavy weight of the Stalinist traditions. These are not yet dead. But there is also the constant, though often latent, struggle between dogma and unfettered thought; and the struggle goes on in every field of intellectual activity. What the Stalinist dogmatism has meant perhaps only those who have experienced it can fully realize. Suffice it to say that in the course of many years Einstein's name was simply unmentionable. Of course, scholars with a knowledge of foreign languages half-stealthily studied his work; but officially it might never have existed. Freud was, and still is, under a ban. For decades Russia lived in intellectual as well as political isolation; isolationism was a virtue. The world outside was an infested, horror-inspiring waste, breathing hostility and heresy; it was safest to avert one's gaze from it. Much of contemporary world literature was a sealed and contaminated book, just as was any Russian writing that did not conform to the canons of 'socialist realism'.

Obviously in this frame of mind the study of philosophy was reduced to scholastical mummery, to chewing over a few sacred texts, and to polemical distortion of the whole development of philosophical ideas. This was all the more grotesque because the Soviet school, even in the Stalin era, did, as I have said, arouse in the pupil the thirst for philosophical conceptions and ideas; but then it tried to quench that thirst with a dehydrated version of dialectical materialism. History fared even worse, especially the history of modern Russia and of the

Russian revolution. The gigantic falsification of that history, which in the interest of the Stalin cult went on for several decades, is familiar enough. So massive was it and so hermetic was it supposed to be that many came to doubt whether any reflex of critical intelligence could have survived underneath.

I have never thought that the falsification has been quite so hermetic and quite so effective; and I have never doubted that the reaction against it would set in. It has set in. The middle 1950s brought a tremendous revolt, open or veiled, against the controls, the censorship, the restrictions and prohibitions of the Stalin era. This revolt has not yet spent its force. The reaction against the Stalinist dogmatism is still developing in constant conflict with the conservatism of a ruling group nearly all the members of which have been brought up in the Stalinist school of thought.

The present situation is thus characterized by a growing demand for freedom of thought and expression on the one hand, and, on the other, by the desire of the ruling group to circumscribe that freedom and to save what can be saved of the canons and taboos of Stalinism. In this conflict at least one factor has definitely favoured the growth of freedom: the spreading awareness that intellectual freedom is a pre-requisite of national efficiency. The need for efficiency, industrial and social, is the greatest single ally of the Soviet universities. It is in the nature of things that freedom should have gained much more ground in science than in the humanities. Einstein's name has at last been placed on the roll of honour; one comes across serious, undogmatic discussions of the philosophy of science with special reference to the theory of relativity. It is in science also that the reaction against intellectual isolationism and an eagerness to learn and assimilate ideas of non-Soviet thinkers and to exchange experiences with them have shown themselves first and foremost.

In the humanities the outlook has remained less encouraging. Here dogma, though bedraggled and humbled, shuffles on. But it can hardly do so for long. The contrast between freedom in science and the lack of it in the humanities is too striking to last. In the long run thought cannot remain half-free and half-slave. Even in the humanities there is a great gap between orthodox appearances and realities. The French once formed the distinction between *le pays réel* and *le pays légal* to describe such a gap in their politics. In the Soviet Union, too, there now exists a 'real country' which is very different from the 'legal' realm of officialdom. People in fact think and argue far more freely and audaciously than one can judge from official statements and curricula and even from so-called scholarly papers.

In economics, where the needs of efficiency cannot be ignored, there has been some revival of theoretical discussion, a little of which is reflected in the periodicals but most of which has been going on unofficially. A great deal of this discussion must, I am afraid, remain unintelligible to Western students trained in the economics of Marshall or even Keynes, because it is conducted in terms of Marxist theory. Here is one more reason, a severely practical one, why Western universities should at last begin to encourage serious and first-hand study of Marx's work. You cannot understand the present Russian economic debates and planning practices without knowing *Das Kapital*.

Generally speaking, this intellectual ferment presents

itself to me as a prelude or pointer towards a renascence of Marxist thought. A pointer, a prelude, a promise— nothing more yet, but nothing less either. It should not be imagined that the intellectual reaction against Stalinism is also a reaction against Marxism. This may have been so in Hungary and Poland in 1956, but in this respect—allow me to repeat this—the situation is very different in the Soviet Union. No doubt there, too, the young and even middle generations have hardly ever known Marxism in any form other than that of its Stalinist corruption; and so there too it has probably been inevitable that in some part the revulsion against Stalinism should rebound on Marxism. But in the Soviet Union anti-Marxism (and anti-Leninism) appears to have remained on the fringe of the intellectual life not merely of the *pays légal* but of the *pays réel*. Marxism has entered into the very core of the national consciousness; and as that consciousness grows more educated, complex, and subtle, it rejects the Marxism of the *pays légal*, the orthodoxy and the ritual; and it rediscovers Marxism the *Weltanschauung* and the critical school of thought which had absorbed and blended the best traditions of Western philosophy and radical political thought.

I do not think, however, that the outcome of this ferment will be merely a restoration of Marxism to its pre- or early-revolutionary virtues. What is going to emerge is probably a new phase in the development of Marxism as free from dogmatism as the pristine Marxism was—or even freer—but immensely enriched by new experience and able to comprehend and interpret it. But here I am perhaps running too far ahead and indulging in what may still be only a fond intellectual hope. But it is true that whatever its mutations Marxism remains the mainstream of Soviet thought.

We should not allow ourselves to be misled on this point by a novel like *Doctor Zhivago*, with its vaguely anti-Marxist message. Whatever his literary merits or de-merits, Pasternak speaks for a generation which is making its exit and whose attitude towards life is not, in my view, that of younger people. To the mood of the latter a story like *The Trial Begins* . . ., written by an unknown Soviet author and recently published outside Russia, seems much closer. And there exists in Russia a large body of submerged or half-submerged literature that is bound to come to the surface presently— a literature which does not repudiate the Bolshevik revolution but seeks to purify its heritage and express its meaning in a new manner. Perhaps the most characteristic *motif* that appears in these writings is the problem of 'three Soviet generations': the grandparents, the much buffeted Old Bolsheviks and veterans of the revolution; their middle-aged sons, the bureaucratically deformed and cowed generation of the Stalin era; and the rebellious grandsons. These last, as they come into conflict with their bureaucrat-fathers, find themselves in moral concord with their old Bolshevik grandparents, who appear archaic at times, as they are bound to, but whose still living faith and fire communicate themselves to the young and strike sparks in them. This 'alliance of the two generations' is not merely a *motif* in fiction; it is a fact of life. Probably nothing gives the ruling group as much anxiety as does this link-up of the very old and the very young, of those who have never quite reconciled themselves to the orthodoxy and priesthood of Stalinism, and of those who have not had the time to become imbued

34

with that orthodoxy and have witnessed its collapse at the very threshold of their adult life.

In literature the corrupt middle generation is fighting to preserve its predominance. Sycophancy is its second nature and 'socialist realism' its artistic canon. The requirements of that canon still have their baneful effects on letters and the arts, although even these effects may not be quite as evil as are the cheapness and the emptiness of our own mass literature and the hopelessness that pervades so much of even the best Western writing. The dictates of socialist realism are less peremptory than they used to be; but baneful they still are.

The conflict between residual Stalinism and the demand for truth and free expression can be observed at its sharpest in historical writing. Here, too, things have improved. Russia's pre-revolutionary history is no longer treated in the spirit of chauvinistic megalomania and xenophobia that prevailed in Stalin's last years. The history of other countries is being taught more soberly and realistically and with far greater respect for their achievements and cultural heritage. There is even a revival of genuine internationalism. The historian's horizon, which used to be centred on Europe, has significantly widened to include Asia, Africa, and other continents. Current political preoccupation with the problems of the entire Soviet bloc and of the underdeveloped nations has promoted this fresh and fruitful curiosity for the destinies of those nations.

Paradoxically, it is the history of the Bolshevik revolution and the Soviet Union that is still the object of wholesale falsification. It may not be easy for some historians to restore historical truth after decades of suppression and distortion. But given time and access to sources and archives, the young historians could certainly accomplish the work. They still run into barriers set up in the interest of the ruling group which does not want to see full light shed on the last forty years. Khrushchev and the men around him are, as I have pointed out, Stalin's epigones; having made their careers under him and having willy-nilly been the accomplices of his crimes, they must, in order to maintain themselves in power, keep the records out of the public eye and mind. At the Twentieth Congress they lifted a corner of the veil and gave a stimulus to intense research. But then they took fright, muzzled the bolder and the more enterprising historians, and produced a new official version of Bolshevik history. This is less crude than Stalin's; but it is still false, and it is still the only authorized and infallible version. At this stage, too, everything is contradiction and everything is provisional. The next political shake-up is bound to entail another great stirring of the historical conscience and another great airing of the annals of the revolution, for nowhere in the world are history and politics and the social conscience as inextricably bound up as they are in the Soviet Union.

To approach my general theme from yet another angle, one may take the recent debate on Soviet law. This was concerned not with technicalities but with the foundations and the philosophy of law and its social and moral implications. The debate arose out of the reform of the criminal code which is still in progress. The reform is to sanction the dismantlement of the old terror machines, the curtailment of the powers of the political police, and the establishment of the 'rule of law'. Opposed attitudes have clashed almost openly: the 'conservatives' have aimed at keeping the reform within the narrowest possible limits, while a 'liberal' school of thought has sought to enlarge the area of freedom and to put into the code as many legal obstacles as possible to any recrudescence of the police state. The debate has centred on such issues as the procedures of a fair and open legal trial and the defendant's rights. Under the old code, of Vyshinsky's ill-famed inspiration, the legal trial, especially in political cases, was based on the presumption of the defendant's guilt. That code has now been denounced as an outrage to justice. The presumption of guilt has been recognized as a monstrosity and abandoned. But the question arose whether in the new code it should be replaced by the presumption of the defendant's innocence, the presumption found in the modern bourgeois law of the West.

In December 1958 the debate seemed to have ended in a compromise. The guiding principles of the new code were adopted; and these contained neither the presumption of guilt nor the presumption of innocence. It was argued that the one was as false as the other, that the court should have no *a priori* presumptions and should be left to resolve questions of innocence or guilt entirely in the light of accumulating evidence. At this compromise, it seemed, matters were to rest. Yet, although the argument against any *a priori* presumption sounded convincing in itself, matters have not in fact been allowed to rest at that. A year after the promulgation of the new code, the issue is again under debate. Even official opinion seems in the meantime to have turned in favour of the presumption of innocence.

The significance of this must be seen in the light of the preceding debate. A year ago it was argued that the presumption of innocence was a peculiarity of the bourgeois liberal law formed at a time when the Western bourgeoisie was struggling against the absolutist monarchy and was anxious to safeguard the rights and liberties of the individual. According to this view, the presumption of innocence was historically vindicated as a weapon in the hands of the progressive middle classes against tyrannical authority; but it was not justified in strict legal theory; and it was out of place in a socialist régime. That was a double-edged argument, however. It gave rise to this question: if the presumption of innocence, whatever the abstract legal arguments against it, helped the bourgeoisie to safeguard its civil liberties against absolutism, should it not also be used, after the experience of Stalinist absolutism, to safeguard the liberties of workers and peasants? It has been difficult for the *pays légal* to get away from this question; and so a year after the debate was ostensibly closed, the authoritative *Kommunist* has spoken up in favour of the presumption of innocence. The argument is not yet concluded; but its bearing on the moral and political climate of the Soviet Union needs no underlining.

Watching this flux of ideas, one is reminded of the intellectual ferment that spread in Europe when medieval scholasticism was collapsing and making way for the Renaissance and the flourishing of rationalist thought. What the Soviet Union is going through now is still an interval between two epochs, an interlude in which the oppressive fogs of the past are still present, but in which one can already sense a breath of the future.

The last decades of Soviet history have been full of unparalleled advance and achievement and also unparalleled oppression and suffering. Hardly any other nation has ever lived through an experience so gigantic,

at once so contradictory and so intense in its contradictions. This makes for an extraordinary richness of thought
and feeling and for high creative tension in the nation's
mind. The sense of that tension permeates the Soviet
Union; watching the horizon one gets the feeling of the
approach of momentous changes, of the approach of
something like an historic act of birth. Russia is once
again pregnant with new, world-shaking thoughts and
ideas. When the present interlude is over, we shall, I
am convinced, witness another flowering of the Russian
intellect and culture, a flowering worthy of the traditions
of Mendeleyev and Pavlov, of Tolstoy, Dostoyevsky
and Chekhov, of Plekhanov, Lenin and Trotsky—a
flowering which will surpass these traditions, and in
which the world as well as the Soviet Union will rejoice.

III

FOREIGN POLICY

I T is a truism that the foreign policy of any government is the prolongation of its domestic policy. But this truth is not as simple as it appears. When a government's domestic policy pursues conflicting purposes its prolongation in foreign affairs cannot be in a straight line; and while domestic policy is shaped primarily by internal pressures, the course of foreign policy depends on the actions and reactions of other governments and on the international balance of power. We should therefore in discussing Soviet foreign policy try and keep in mind the interplay of all these factors. We may begin by asking how the recent changes within the Soviet Union have affected the conduct of foreign affairs. We should then examine the relations between the U.S.S.R. and its partners in the Soviet bloc. And finally, we will survey the relationship between the Soviet Union and the West, and relate foreign policy to the international balance of power.

That the changes within the Soviet Union have altered the manner and the style in which its diplomacy defends its interests abroad is evident. Gone are the grimness, the awe-inspiring secretiveness, and the back-handed abruptness with which Soviet diplomacy acted only a few years ago. Gone is the Kremlin-immured autocrat's contempt for public opinion. A government which is more sensitive than Stalin's to popular moods at home is also more sensitive to them abroad. True, there does not yet exist in the U.S.S.R. any vocal public opinion able to express itself critically on the official conduct of foreign affairs. But there is a semi-articulate popular feeling strong enough to be sensed by the government. The Soviet people undoubtedly viewed with distrust Stalin's autocratic irresponsibility in his dealings with foreign powers, even if they approved of much of his foreign policy. The thoughtful resented the fact that he kept his most important diplomatic moves a secret from his own nation. By contrast, Khrushchev gives the appearance of taking the people into his confidence and this assures his diplomacy of a strong popular backing.

Much has recently been said in the West about the Soviet people's desire for peace. This desire was, I think, quite as strong under Stalin and even he could not ignore it. No doubt he played on nationalist emotions and in his last years tried to whip up an intense xenophobia which usually goes with war hysteria. But he did not have much success in this. Even a totalitarian propaganda could not whip up any war hysteria in a nation that had just suffered a cruel invasion, had lost 20 million men in war, and had seen many of its cities and towns burned and razed to the ground. Recent years have brought a reaction against the Great Russian chauvinism and megalomania of the early 1950s; and intense though the popular pride in Soviet achievements has been, this is tempered by a sense of national modesty and dignity. It is to the credit of Khrushchev's government that, on the whole, it has not tried to exploit the sputniks and luniks in order to foster a mood of arrogance and aggressiveness, a mood which, unfortunately, was not absent from the West during the years of the American monopoly in atomic power. Nor has Moscow so far been seized by a panicky fear that Western spies, real or imaginary, were stealing its technological secrets.

The effect of popular pacifism on official policy is powerfully reinforced by pressure for more consumer goods. Yielding to it, the government has had to revise repeatedly its economic plans, especially the housing programmes, and to divert resources from armament to civilian production. The pressure for consumer goods is not likely to slacken; it may yet compel the government to revise its plans even further. Of course, when the national income and the national product are rapidly growing, an increased output of consumer goods may be quite compatible with increased armament. Whether they are in fact compatible depends on just how strong is the pressure for consumer goods and on the tempo of the arms race. If both grow beyond a certain point, they are bound to come into conflict. The Soviet government has therefore every reason to try and call a halt to the arms race and to strive for an agreed international reduction of armaments. No government would be more popular in the Soviet Union than one that succeeded in this.

The pacifist temper of the Soviet masses and their manifest eagerness for contact with the West should not, however, be interpreted as signs of any sympathy with 'Western capitalism', or of any fundamental opposition to the social system of the U.S.S.R. Such an attitude may perhaps be found among a small and scattered minority. On the whole, the last few years have enhanced and deepened what may be described as the socialist consciousness of the masses. After Khrushchev's revelations about Stalin, many have learned to view their rulers with critical, even cynical, eyes; but this has not weakened the people's basic allegiance to the 'workers' state'. I should like to repeat that we should not in this respect confuse the situation in the Soviet Union with conditions prevailing in Hungary, in Poland, or Eastern Germany. The Russians have lived under a revolution which was not imposed on them by a foreign conqueror, but was the authentic product of their own national destinies. Under the governments which inherited the October Revolution they have become the world's second industrial power, and achieved the greatest military and international triumphs of their history. Communism, such as it is, has become the 'ruling idea' of the Soviet Union, just as liberalism is the ruling British idea, and 'freedom of private enterprise and initiative' the American. The popular pacifism, far from being in conflict with the communist consciousness, is permeated by it. Probably no nation lives in greater horror of nuclear war than do the Russians, and no nation is as determined to defend its social system and, if need be, to fight for it.

It is worthwhile realizing that even the eager desire of the Soviet people for free and unhampered contacts with the West is not altogether free of resentment and suspicion. The Soviet people view the West through the prism of their own experience. To them 'the West', naturally enough, includes Germany, which only recently was Hitler's Germany. They remember, of course, that against Hitler they fought in alliance with the Atlantic nations. But many also recall how long they had to wait before their Western allies opened up the second front in Europe. Many remember the abrupt cessation by the United States of Lend-Lease Aid at the conclusion of the war, and the subsequent Western embargoes on trade with Russia. They have never ceased to suspect that all this was part of a strategy designed first to let the Soviet Union bleed itself white in the war and then to prevent or delay its recovery. They remember the time when U.S. generals and politicians, made over-confident by an ephemeral monopoly in atomic weapons, threatened to 'roll back' Soviet power. They see a ring of American bases still surrounding the Soviet bloc and German military power rising from the ashes and being transformed into N.A.T.O.'s spearhead. Even if they know or guess that Stalin had all too often needlessly provoked the West and produced hostility, they still wonder to what extent capitalism remains dangerously hostile towards the Soviet Union, because it is jealous of communist progress and fearful of its own prospects. They watch hopefully Khrushchev's diplomacy. As they see it, he has been trying hard to make good Stalin's and Molotov's mistakes. His approach and language are reasonably conciliatory; he has cut down the size of the Soviet Union's armed forces; he was the first to stop nuclear tests; he has wound up some of the Soviet military bases abroad; he took the initiative to evacuate Austria; he has exerted himself to stop the civil war in Indo-China; he has, despite opposition at home and many snubs from abroad, stubbornly persisted in his attempts to renew contacts with the leaders of the West; and he has been to the United States to proclaim the Soviet Union's desire for peace and to produce what they believe to be *the* master scheme of international dis-armament. They now watch anxiously to see the result of Khrushchev's initiatives. If he achieves nothing, they will be confirmed in their worst suspicions of the West;

and for all their pacific mood they would not like their government to surrender any of its vital interests.

From a somewhat different angle, Soviet foreign policy, and the popular mood behind it, may be seen as compounded of a large residuum of Stalinist isolationism and of a new and growing internationalism. I know that to speak of Stalin's isolationism in this context is to cause some raising of eyebrows. The prevalent Western view of Stalin's foreign policy is determined by the last phase of that policy, when Soviet armies marched into many countries and carried revolution abroad on the point of the bayonet. It should not be forgotten, however, that of the three decades of the Stalin era, more than two passed under the sign of Socialism in a Single Country, which was nothing but a doctrine of isolationism expressed in the Bolshevik idiom. This was, of course, a brand of isolationism very different from its American counterpart: the isolationist United States was separated from the main storm centres of world politics by two oceans, whereas Russia's frontiers lay open to any invader. The American isolationism grew out of security and self-sufficiency, while the Russian grew out of insecurity, fear, and absorption in the reconstruction of Soviet society. The dominant motive of Stalin's foreign policy in the 1920s and the 1930s, when the memories of revolution, foreign intervention, and of the Leninist commitment to world revolution were still fresh, was to avoid any dangerous involvement in foreign class struggles and foreign conflicts between revolution and counter-revolution. The victory of Soviet arms in the Second World War and the Chinese revolution undermined this attitude; and so in its last phase, Stalin's foreign policy was an implicit negation of the idea that had inspired it, of Socialism in a Single Country. The Soviet bloc, comprising China and nearly all the countries of Eastern Europe, came into being. Even then Stalin still tried to impose an isolationist pattern on that bloc and to subordinate the interests and aspirations of all its members to the sacred egoism of the first 'workers' state', the Soviet Union. He produced a parody of a Socialist Empire, in which China and the nations of Eastern Europe were to be both the proud builders of socialism and Moscow's wretched colonies.

This 'Socialist Empire' has not survived Stalin. What has undone it is the reaction against isolationism and the stirring of an internationalist mood in the Soviet Union; and a revulsion in China and in most of Eastern Europe against the sacred egoism of the first 'workers' state'. It is still too early perhaps to gauge the full strength of the new internationalism, but its influence is undeniable and it has shown itself most strongly in Soviet relations with the other members of the Soviet bloc.

I have said that Soviet foreign policy is made up of a residuum of the Stalinist isolationism and of the new internationalism. In this respect foreign policy is indeed a prolongation of domestic policy. Both within and without the Soviet Union Khrushchevism represents an uneasy balance between Stalinist traditions and the revulsion against them. The persistence of a residual isolationism is not merely a matter of inertia. It results also from the facts of the international situation. In a world split between rival power blocs, each bloc is up to a point bound to remain isolated from the other, and in each the strongest Power seeks to safeguard for itself the prerogatives of leadership. But here as in domestic policy it is the interplay of the old and the new that matters.

The Soviet leaders have undertaken an attempt to transform Stalin's 'Socialist Empire' into something like a socialist commonwealth. They have given up Stalin's ambition to control directly the economic and political life of the countries of the Soviet bloc. They have disbanded the Soviet-Chinese, Soviet-Hungarian, Soviet-Rumanian, Soviet-Bulgarian and other Joint Stock Companies through which Stalin had penetrated the key industries of those countries and acquired controlling interests in them. Stalin dictated the terms of trade between the Soviet Union and the other members of the Soviet bloc, terms which were often unfairly advantageous to the Soviet Union. Stalin's successors have done much to compensate Poland, China, Eastern Germany, and others, for the losses they suffered thereby and have helped them with generous economic aid. Khrushchev has even committed himself to the long-term task of equalizing the distribution of wealth throughout the Soviet bloc—this is the meaning of his doctrinal thesis that all countries of that bloc 'should achieve the building of communism more or less simultaneously'. In view of the great disparities of economic development in the Soviet bloc, such equalization of wealth can at best be only a long-term objective. Even so, the fact that Khrushchev has had to commit his government to it, shows that the influence of the new internationalism is far from negligible. Against this must be set the inertia of Stalinism, which showed itself, for instance, when the ideological conflict between Moscow and Belgrade flared up once again in the spring of 1958, and the Soviet government resorted to some economic reprisals.

Within the Soviet bloc as within the Soviet Union

itself there is a striking contrast between reform and progress in economic and social policy and a timid conservatism in politics. The Hungarian rising marked a turning point here too: it strengthened the conservative tendency. At the time of the Twentieth Congress, Moscow virtually gave up its claims to ideological infallibility and supremacy in the communist camp. Khrushchev proclaimed the right of every country to choose its own road to socialism. Moscow was reconciled with Tito; the old heresy hunts were abandoned; the Rajk trial was declared null and void; and Gomulka and Nagy were being rehabilitated. Togliatti, the leader of the Italian Communist Party, went so far as to proclaim the end of the era during which Moscow had been the sole leading centre of international communism; he hailed the advent of an era of 'polycentrism'. But then, with the civil war in Hungary, the anti-Stalinist tide began to ebb. Khrushchev launched the campaign against revisionism, and declared that not every 'road to socialism' a nation might choose was good, and that, indeed, the Hungarian road led not to socialism but back to capitalism. He reasserted the Soviet claim to ideological supremacy and to the leading role within the bloc. He followed this up by another excommunication of Titoism and Nagy's execution was a reminder of the strength of the Stalinist tradition.

But here too Khrushchevism has not gone back all the way to Stalinism. It has retreated only half the way to an intermediate position. Moscow has not reasserted its claim to leadership in the old categorical and inflexible manner; and to make its leadership secure it relies on Soviet economic and political preponderance rather than on political coercion and ideological dictation. The 'different roads to socialism' are still something more than a mere catch phrase. Whether any communist government within the Soviet bloc is really free to choose its road depends on that government's strength and courage; Mao is altogether his own master; Gomulka's situation is ambiguous. The degree of orthodoxy prevailing within the communist parties varies from country to country—the old 'monolith' can hardly be recreated.

Under the surface an economic process has been in motion which is of the greatest significance: within the Soviet bloc international division of labour is becoming the guiding principle of economic policy. It is in this that the new internationalism manifests itself most markedly. Trade between the Soviet Union and its allies has been growing rapidly, and its terms are increasingly advantageous to the Chinese and the Eastern Europeans. A 'communist common market' has come into being. What is even more important is that the 'international division of labour' is spreading from trade to industry, from the circulation of goods to production. In the last few years the Committee for Economic Mutual Assistance (on which all the East European communist governments are represented, with the Chinese present as observers) has begun to act as an international planning authority. It has produced detailed schemes of specialization and co-ordination for the various industries of these countries; it has worked to link up and adjust the various national plans now in operation, and to prepare an overall long-term plan for the joint development of the economic resources of the Soviet Union and Eastern Europe. Important decisions have been taken about the distribution or redistribution of production, for instance in engineering, throughout the Soviet Union and Eastern Europe.

This work is still in one of its initial phases; but its clear purpose is to integrate the economic structures of the Soviet Union and of Eastern Europe, to break down the national barriers and to build up an organization that will gradually supersede the economic entities of the various nation-states. No doubt such an endeavour would arouse bitter opposition and inflame the nationalism of the small nations, if it were to be modelled on an imperialist pattern, if the division of labour favoured the strong and handicapped the weak, if it reserved the development of, say, heavy engineering for the Soviet Union and reduced its partners to specialization in primary production and light industry. This, however, does not so far appear to have been the spirit or the purpose of the scheme—but rather a balanced promotion of both primary production and manufacturing, and light and heavy industry in all communist-ruled countries. Provided that these measures and plans do not in fact discriminate against the small nations and provided that they are sufficiently well balanced to avoid grave disproportions between needs and production, and between the various branches of industry, they should indeed lead to a more or less painless overcoming of national sovereignties in the economic field and to the emergence of an international Union of the first magnitude. Even now there are no tariff walls, there is no fear of commercial competition, and there are only very few protectionist interests at work within the Soviet bloc. If the process of integration were to embrace, as Moscow hopes it will, China too, then the Soviet bloc would form in the last quarter of this century, a single economic entity and a common 'market' four or five times larger than the North American market and at least twice as large as a common American and Western European market would be. Within an economic entity of that size technological progress, productivity, standardization and mass production could develop on a scale never hitherto seen.

This prospect decisively influences the general conduct of Soviet foreign affairs. To secure the uninterrupted growth of this 'socialist commonwealth' and to ensure stability for all its constituent governments is the paramount objective of Soviet policy. In this matter Soviet diplomacy acts on behalf not only of the Soviet Union, but of the entire bloc. An international *détente* and a substantial reduction in the burden of armaments would, of course, create the favourable conditions of growth; and it is with this in mind that Khrushchev speaks of the need to preserve the international *status quo* and makes this the main plank of his diplomatic programme.

What does 'the preservation of the *status quo*' amount to? What Khrushchev speaks of is the formal, geographical–political *status quo*; he would like to stabilize the existing configuration of frontiers, including the boundary that cuts across Germany. The preservation of this, however, need not be at all identical with the preservation of the actual *status quo* in the international balance of power. Indeed, Khrushchev makes it no secret that on the basis of the formal *status quo* he expects the balance of power to shift in favour of the Soviet Union.

But how sincere, one is often asked, is the Soviet desire to respect at least the formal *status quo*? Can the Soviet government be trusted to refrain from aggression? Will it not, circumstances permitting, seek to dominate

Western Germany? Is the urge for conquest not inherent in communism and Soviet power politics? Such questions, based on the experience of imperialist conquest, were still partly relevant to Stalin's policy; but they bear, in my view, little or no relation to the new phase of Soviet diplomacy and to its power-political background.

Foreign conquest has usually aimed at increasing a conqueror's economic and/or military power either by opening up for him new markets, sources of raw materials, and reserves of cheap labour, or by putting him in command of strategically vital positions. As a rule, foreign expansion also helped to overcome or to compensate slowness or impediments in the development of domestic resources. This was still the motive of Stalin's policy after the Second World War: he sought to dominate the countries of Eastern and Central Europe and laid his hands on their resources at a time when the Soviet economy was shattered by war and the prospects of its recovery were highly uncertain.

This situation obviously belongs to the past. To be sure, Stalin's successors cannot and will not preside over the liquidation of the communist régimes in Eastern Europe. But they have no need or desire to go back to Stalin's method of conquest. The Soviet Union has now in its planned economy a means of increasing its power far more rapidly and securely than by conquest. With every year or two of industrial development it is adding to its resources more than it could possibly gain by the subjugation of any medium-sized European nation. If the targets of the present Seven Year Plan are reached, the U.S.S.R. will, by 1965, have added to its present economic potential nearly twice the potential of Western Germany. This is precisely why the Soviet Union is altering in its favour the balance of power, without changing the formal *status quo*.

This new strength, however, is not invulnerable. Its vulnerability lies in the communist régimes of Eastern Europe. The preservation of the *status quo* should, in Khrushchev's intentions, shield those régimes. As the Russians see it, the present division of spheres of influence in Europe may be upset either on the initiative of the Western Powers or by the internal disruption of some communist régime in Eastern Europe or by a combination of both. That the Western Powers should still try to 'roll back' communism may be ruled out in theory. But the recurrence of dangerous crises in Eastern Europe, such as the Berlin and Budapest risings of 1953 and 1956, cannot be ruled out; and this may, under certain circumstances, still lead to Western intervention. In the face of another Berlin rising, accompanied by unrest in Eastern Germany, a rearmed Federal German Republic might not remain as passive as it was in 1953; and the involvement of West German forces in any fighting along the East German boundary might involve the other N.A.T.O. Powers, especially if their troops continue to be stationed in Berlin. Soviet policy in Stalin's days was haunted by the fear of such a development; and Khrushchev's policy is not free from that fear. Stalin tried to force a Western withdrawal from Berlin by means of the 1948 blockade. After an interval of ten years Khrushchev set out to achieve the withdrawal by means of negotiations. Berlin remains the Achilles' heel of the Soviet bloc.

But—such is the dialectic of the situation—Berlin is also the Achilles' heel of the West. From the Soviet standpoint the preservation of the *status quo* (i.e. the security of communist Eastern Europe) requires that the Western enclave be eliminated from Berlin. From the Western viewpoint, this precisely would upset the *status quo*. If Soviet diplomacy seeks to insure the Soviet bloc against the tremors that a turbulent Berlin might yet send through Eastern Europe, the West is afraid that its withdrawal from Berlin would send no less dangerous tremors through N.A.T.O. and induce the Germans (and others) to begin to reconcile themselves to Soviet supremacy in Europe. None of these fears is just a figment of a frightened imagination; both sides have enough ground to be afraid. The result is a stalemate of fears.

However, the *status quo* may be upset not only in Berlin and in Europe; it may be disrupted by the growth of revolutionary ferment in Asia and Africa as well. This has its own momentum which is up to a point independent of the policies of the Great Powers. The Soviet attitude towards the anti-imperialist movement there is by no means clear cut. In so far as that movement weakens the West, Moscow has reason enough to encourage it. But when it tends to upset the international *status quo*, Moscow is afraid. Despite the fact that Khrushchev threatened to send Soviet volunteers to fight in Egypt during the Suez war and repeated the threat during the Iraq and Lebanon crises in 1958, nothing would have suited him less than a conflagration in the Middle East which might have spread. There is also the fact that under the leadership of men like Nasser and Kassem Arab nationalism has been a highly unreliable ally of the Soviet Union—it is indeed half ally and half enemy. Yet Moscow has been wary of attempts at undermining the bourgeois leadership of Arab nationalism and bringing the movement under communist guidance.

In Iraq the Communist Party was the chief driving force of the 1958 revolution; and according to most Western observers on the spot it was quite capable of seizing power. Yet it has not even tried to do so. Khrushchev's policy in the Middle East has been almost a replica of Stalin's policy in China in 1925–27, when Stalin considered Chiang Kai-shek as his ally and urged the Chinese Communist Party to accept Chiang's leadership and submit to Kuomintang discipline. Khrushchev has similarly induced the communists of Iraq to acknowledge unconditionally General Kassem as their 'national leader'; he has even blamed them for having at one time 'allowed themselves to be carried away by the tide of revolution'. He has also called a halt to the campaign against Nasser which the communists had begun.

In taming Middle Eastern communism Khrushchev has acted in the interest of the *status quo*. His policy has undoubtedly resulted in a relative easing of the international tension in the Middle East. But no one knows how long this may last. The upheaval has hardly spent all its momentum; sooner or later it may once again take on violent forms and upset all plans based on the *status quo*. Even if the relatively calm interval is prolonged, revolutionary situations may arise elsewhere in Asia (and Africa) and destroy the present utterly precarious equilibrium.

One factor may become important in this connexion: Red China's evident reluctance to endorse Khrushchev's diplomacy wholeheartedly and accept the preservation of the *status quo* as the objective of its own policy. Outlawed by the West, China has no reason to strive for the international settlement advocated by Khrushchev; and to the fresh revolutionary fervour of the Chinese, preserving the *status quo* may not appear to be at all a desirable objective.

Divergencies between Peking and Moscow may affect the attitudes of the communist parties of India, Indo-China, and adjacent countries. In India, potentially the next and most important battlefield in the class struggle, the Communist Party has not so far followed the example the Chinese set in their long struggle against the Kuomintang, when for years they challenged Chiang Kai-shek's government from Yenan and other bases. The Indian communists have so far shown little or no inclination to adopt so offensive a strategy. Despite wide popular backing, they have given up their Kerala base without effective resistance; and they have refrained from defying Nehru's authority. They appear to adjust their tactics to Khrushchev's policy rather than to the Chinese pattern of revolution. The same seems to be true of the Indonesian Communist Party which has, despite its very great strength, accepted Soekarno's leadership. All over that area Khrushchev acts as the guardian of the *status quo*; and he, rather than Mao Tse-tung, appears to set the line for the communist parties there.

But revolutionary situations may yet develop over which Moscow may lose control, as it lost control over the Chinese revolution in 1948–49. It is impossible to foresee the course of developments, but it is clear that the *status quo* may be exposed to many hazards.

I have said that Soviet diplomacy seeks to 'freeze' the present demarcation lines between the two blocs. For how long? Perhaps for a decade, perhaps for longer. The Soviet Union is out to gain another ten or fifteen years, in the course of which it intends to prepare for the decisive and open contest with the West. Let me explain what I mean by an 'open contest'. This need not be a test of arms. In a struggle between opposed social systems, Marxists hold, that system is bound to win which is superior in efficiency, in the ability to deploy society's productive forces and to unfold men's creative energies. Until recently the Soviet Union was bound to be defeated if it submitted to any such test. The Russian revolution was in danger, as Trotsky once put it, of being defeated by an 'invasion of cheap foreign goods', if not by armed invasion. The whole Bolshevik policy of the last forty years aimed at avoiding or postponing such a test. Stalin's isolationism, protectionism, and iron curtain were designed to keep the danger at bay, to keep the Soviet people immune from the impact of higher Western efficiency and higher Western standards of living.

With the growth of Soviet industrial power the need for that protectionism has been vanishing. The time is not far off when capitalist countries may begin to fear the 'invasion of cheap goods' from the Soviet Union. No doubt the 'Soviet challenge' still contains an ingredient of bluff. American wealth is still far greater and so, in many respects, is American efficiency. The Soviet Union is not quite ready yet for any *open* economic competition with the West. It is still shielding itself against Western superiority; it still relies on devices of 'socialist protectionism'. But this era is drawing to a close. Within the coming decade, we know, the Soviet Union hopes to achieve economic parity with the United States; it expects that by 1965 the Soviet bloc will produce more than half of the world's industrial output. Whether these expectations are fulfilled a few years earlier or later, the Soviet Union is, in any case, likely to realize its ambition by the time this quarter of the century has passed. And once the Soviet Union has achieved this, it will be interested in conducting its contest with the West on the basis of international *laissez-faire*. It will then be able to adopt a policy of Open Doors, open doors for capitalism and communism alike, open doors in the countries of the Soviet bloc and the non-communist world, because Open Doors will automatically favour the wealthier and the more efficient of the antagonists. Only then will the Soviet challenge to 'peaceful competition' acquire its full force.

What will be the impact on the Western world? The Soviet leaders believe that the popular appeal of communism will then become irresistible. German, British, and American workers could not be attracted by communism when it was associated with a régime representing lower productivity and lower standards of living than those they had attained under Western capitalism— with a régime which, in addition, was based on the suppression of all political freedom. This association of communism with Russia has been a basic cause of the failure of communism throughout the West during the greater part of this century. In Western Europe the latest important phase in the struggle between communism and anti-communism was resolved, in the years 1945–1950, primarily by the contrast between the economic poverty and the oppressive régime of the U.S.S.R. and the wealth and relative liberalism of the U.S.A., a contrast projected abroad and thrown into relief by Stalin's reparations policy, on the one hand, and by Marshall Aid on the other.

At present, however, communism looks forward to a very different prospect, when its appeal may be as much enhanced by Soviet wealth, technological supremacy, feats of mass education, and a freer régime as the attraction of bourgeois democracy has hitherto been enhanced by the fact that it has had behind it the vast material and moral resources of the United States. By the time of the next great social crisis in Western Europe (provided that the crisis does not develop 'prematurely'), communism may hope to overcome its isolation, to sap the influence of the anti-communist parties, and to place itself at the head of the peoples. The impact on Asia and Africa may work more powerfully and swiftly. It was this prospect that at the Twentieth Congress induced Khrushchev and Mikoyan to speak, in defiance of the Leninist tradition, about the possibilities of a 'peaceful transition from capitalism to socialism'—a transition achieved without civil war—in various countries. It is this prospect also which provides the Soviet leaders with the ideological justification for striving to 'preserve the *status quo*' and to gain time for the Soviet bloc—to gain it from the Western Powers in the first instance, but also from the communist movements outside the Soviet bloc.

In effect Khrushchev tells the communists of Western Europe, the Middle East, India, and Indonesia: 'There is no need for you to engage immediately in any decisive struggle for power. Wait until *we* have created conditions in which you will be able to resume the struggle for power with the least danger and risk to yourselves and ourselves, conditions in which your victory will be assured.'

What this policy tacitly assumes is, first, that the Western economy will not make much headway in the coming decade or so, or, at any rate, that the pace of its advance will be slack; and, secondly, that the demonstration of superior Soviet efficiency, economic and social, can by itself secure the further ascendancy of communism even in the West, although Khrushchev, naturally enough, does not exactly explain how he expects this to happen. He appears to be aware to some extent that his most 'optimistic' anticipations may come to grief; but on them his policy rests nevertheless. Whether his ultimate prospects are realistic or not, the outcome of the industrial contest between the U.S.S.R. and the U.S.A. will indeed have a decisive influence on the ideological conflict of our age.

But before that stage is reached at least another decade has yet to run its course. Can the international *status quo* be maintained for another decade? Can the world be prevented from plunging into nuclear disaster in the meantime? These are the great question marks suspended over Soviet foreign policy.

I have described the stalemate of fears to which the Great Powers have brought themselves, and I have said that their fears are, unfortunately, no mere figments of their imagination. Ever since the last war both East and West have been mortally frightened of each other and have feverishly piled up arms, nuclear and/or conventional. Now they are afraid of continuing this arms race; but they are equally afraid of calling it off. They live in terror of their own terrors; and they are seized with terror when they think of parting with their terrors. This may be the tragedy of all tragedies—yet how grotesque it seems. East and West confront one another across a gulf, like two men, each standing on top of an avalanche, each afraid of budging lest the avalanche underneath starts moving, each hurling insults across the gulf, each, with a strontium cloud overhead, brandishing his nuclear weapons, and each frightened of climbing down and meeting the adversary on safer ground. And yet both feel that they cannot carry on like this, each fixed on the top of his avalanche, because the avalanches may start rolling of themselves. It is as dangerous for each to remain where he is as it is to try and climb down.

We have watched this stalemate of fears in the conflicts over Berlin; and we see it reflected again in the dilemmas of disarmament. In the years when the United States enjoyed its monopoly of atomic weapons the Soviet Union tried to counterbalance this by maintaining supremacy in conventional arms. Now, when the Soviet Union enjoys a quasi-monopolistic advantage in long-range missiles, the United States and its allies try to neutralize this by clinging to a far-flung but rather old-fashioned, almost conventional, network of military and naval bases. First the Western Powers urged the Soviet Union to give up its superiority in conventional weapons; and the Soviet Union asked the United States to renounce its atom bombs, meanwhile working hard to catch up in nuclear weapons. Now, in turn, Russia is urging N.A.T.O. to wind up its 'conventional' military bases in Europe and Asia; while the United States is all the more anxious to catch up with Russia in long-range rocketry. In every phase of the race the Power in the lead has little or no inducement to yield ground, while the other prefers to postpone any concession and meantime strains every nerve to make good the lag. And so the race goes on to the accompaniment of assurances that the time to stop and seek a settlement will come later, when no one will presumably have to make good any lag. But all the time someone has a lag to make good. And so at every stage of post-war history one side has had to build up 'positions of strength' from which it promises to parley in all earnestness later; yet no sooner has it built them up than the other side turns out to be in command of even more formidable positions. And the furious pace of technological progress renders the successive elements of strength obsolete and almost worthless in no time.

A realization of the futility and horror of this situation seems to underlie the disarmament proposals which Khrushchev has put before the United Nations. His argument for complete disarmament is as simple as the Columbus egg. So far all attempts at partial disarmament have failed, ostensibly because the Powers could not agree over control and inspection. Yet partial disarmament admits only partial inspection, which is inherently inadequate. Under it the Powers cannot allow one another to inspect all their arsenals—they cannot divulge the secrets of those arsenals that are not covered by the disarmament scheme. Yet no Power can be sure that behind the screen of 'legitimate secrecy' the other Power is not evading the obligation to disarm. It is therefore impossible to devise a foolproof scheme for partial inspection. From this Khrushchev draws the conclusion that only complete disarmament can break the vicious circle; it alone admits complete control and inspection; under it, no Power would be entitled to any military secrecy, and this would enable any Power to make sure that there was no evasion.

The West has viewed this Soviet Columbus egg rather sceptically: surely complete disarmament is Utopia? Ground for scepticism is not lacking, unfortunately, if only because neither of the power blocs can be sure that the other would under any circumstances be willing to beat its rockets into ploughs. In any case, complete disarmament must really be a series of partial disarmaments because it cannot physically be carried out at a stroke.

The Soviet proposal provides for the whole process to be carried out in several stages in the course of at least four years. Complete control and inspection would come only with the last and final stage. At the preceding stages there would still be only partial inspection, although the area of inspection would progressively widen. Thus the difficulty which has prevented agreement on partial disarmament reappears in the scheme for complete disarmament. Each of the partners may still have reason to fear that while he is disarming, his potential enemy is not. Accumulated suspicions, rooted in deep conflicts of interests, may render that fear unbearable and may indeed make any radical disarmament scheme look like Utopia. We are back at the top of the two avalanches.

But if the choice is, as it appears to be, between co-existence and co-suicide, between Utopia and mankind's self-annihilation, is it not more courageous, more worthy of the human race—and is it not safer also—to opt for Utopia and to try and make of it a reality?

IV

EAST AND WEST:

IMPLICATIONS OF COEXISTENCE

'PEACEFUL coexistence'—so much has already been said about it that the term has become threadbare. It remains meaningful nevertheless. Whether we are aware of this or not, peaceful coexistence has long been a fact of the international situation. True, twice since the October Revolution attempts have been made to prevent or disrupt coexistence: first, immediately after 1917, when the Western powers intervened in Russia and fought Bolshevism, while Bolshevik Russia believed in the imminence of international revolution; and then during the Second World War, when Nazi Germany refused to 'coexist' with the Soviet Union (and was unable to 'coexist' with the bourgeois democracies of the West either). Apart from these two very important intervals, peaceful coexistence has gone on for decades.

There are, of course, quite a few varieties of coexistence. Antagonistic social systems may confront each other in intense hostility but without resorting to arms; or they may live side by side and ignore each other, although it is difficult to visualize such a situation between régimes the antagonism of which is of a fundamental nature and has assumed world-wide scale. There may be various modalities of coexistence in friendly or hostile neutrality. And, finally, even governments which are ideologically poles apart may co-operate and conclude alliances. In the last forty years we have run through this whole gamut. Following the years of the anti-Bolshevik intervention, there were times, during the late 1920s and early 1930s, when East and West tried to ignore one another and to live in mutual isolation. The Second World War brought the alliance between the Western democracies and Russia. But the alliance was ridden with latent tensions, which subsequently came to the surface and led to the cold war. We have now reached the stage when it becomes more and more difficult and dangerous to persist in this kind of cold war and more and more urgent to find, if possible, an easier and more co-operative relationship.

The Russians declare frankly that they envisage peaceful coexistence as a competitive contest between the opposed social systems, a contest which should be conducted in the economic sphere and by political means but from which war and the threat of war, implied in the present arms race, should be excluded. This is the so-called Soviet challenge to the West. What are its implications, and prospects?

The Soviet Union, we know, is at present the world's second industrial power and it aspires to attain economic parity with the United States and then to become, in a decade or so, the world's wealthiest industrial nation. As the Soviet rate of industrial expansion is now generally recognized to be much higher than the American, it is very probable that the Soviet Union will indeed become the industrial equal of the United States in the relatively near future. Although Soviet standards of living may still remain below the American ten years from now, they are certain to have risen above Western European standards. This will be a tremendous achievement for a people whose standards were not so long ago closer to those of China or India than of Western Europe.

But what is involved here is not merely comparative statistics of production and consumption. The question is not just who will outproduce whom and when. If this were all, the prospect would not have even part of the dramatic tension it obviously has. We would then still have to expect a great shift in the world's balance of power. But similar shifts, on a smaller scale, have occurred in the past, without creating comparable social, political, and ideological problems. Till the close of the nineteenth century Britain was the world's industrial workshop. Then the United States and Germany caught up with her and surpassed her. The shift that is now in progress is different in kind as well as scale. When Germany and the United States caught up industrially with Britain, their success did not place a question mark over the social system prevailing in Britain. The two nations had achieved their ascendancy within a framework of social relationships and institutions very similar to, and largely modelled on, those which had predominated in Britain. On both sides of the Atlantic capitalism was in its heyday. The attainment of industrial maturity by new nations demonstrated only the vitality of bourgeois society and its immense capacity for expansion. Britain was weakened as the world empire; but in her very reverse there triumphed the principle that underlay her organization.

The economic ascendancy of the Soviet Union tends to place a huge question mark over the structure of Western society. Theoretically, the question mark is not new. Socialism at large and Marxism in particular have disputed the rationality of the bourgeois order for more than a century. Even before 1848 Marx and Engels claimed that capitalist enterprise was increasingly impeding the development of productive resources because it could not function without boom and slump and without making the rich richer and the poor poorer. They saw in this the manifestation of the anarchy of capitalism and looked ahead to the time when capitalism would have to give place to a new order based on public ownership and representing a superior social organization. But for over a century this has been, as far as Western society is concerned, abstract theory; the prolonged theoretical onslaught on the 'bastions of capitalism' could not shake them. Whatever its record of exploitation and oppression, whatever the anarchy of its trade cycles and the destructiveness of its wars, Western capitalism has developed its productive resources beyond what either its critics or even its apologists had imagined as possible. The working classes have in varying degrees participated in the resulting benefits and have consequently placed their hopes on reforms within the capitalist system rather than on its revolutionary overthrow.

Even the Russian revolution was unable to change this situation. True, its first victories sent a fever through Western society and aroused a panic in the possessing classes. But subsequently the Russian revolution itself seemed to disprove the Marxist critique of capitalism and to restore the self-confidence of the West. The 'building of socialism' had been initiated in one of the world's most backward and poverty-stricken countries, with the result that for a long time the Bolshevik régime was unable to deliver the goods socialism had promised. The Soviet levels of production remained far below Western levels; and so did the Soviet standards of living, not to speak of the standards of civil liberties. Despite its slumps,

Western capitalism continued by and large to demonstrate its vitality and efficiency, while Russia appeared to provide the evidence of the inefficiency of socialism. (I am here speaking of 'social efficiency' in the broadest sense which includes economic productivity and social and political freedom.) Russia had through the revolution deprived herself of the advantages of capitalism without as yet availing herself of the advantages of socialism.

It is now clear that this was a period of transition. In the fifth decade of the revolution, having undergone forcible industrialization, the Soviet Union is reaping the first benefits of socialism. This at once carries the Marxist critique of bourgeois society from the sphere of theory into that of practice. In the years to come the merits and de-merits of Western social and political institutions are going to be subjected to new and stern scrutiny. The old question of social versus private ownership of the means of production is being re-opened in a new manner. The Soviet inheritors of the Marxist case need no longer argue primarily from the social inefficiency of capitalism *per se*. They may well grant that Western capitalism has proved to possess far greater staying power and adaptability than Marxism had assumed. But they point out that capitalism, even in its most modern and advanced variety, is still proving to be a less efficient form of social organization than is even the not so very advanced socialist or quasi-socialist system of the Soviet Union. They now argue, in other words, that Western capitalism will succumb not so much—or not directly—because of its own crises and inherent contradictions as because of its inability to match the achievements of socialism.

This is how the Marxist argument is at present being re-formulated in the Soviet Union. (For reasons of doctrinal orthodoxy this modification of the Marxist critique of capitalism is being carried out implicitly rather than explicitly.) The argument may still seem far-fetched to people in the West. But its influence on the political thinking of the under-developed nations, who form the majority of the human race, is unmistakable. To them the unparalleled rapidity of the industrial rise of the Soviet Union already suggests that they themselves are more likely to achieve a similar rise on the basis of public rather than private ownership.

But even the wealthiest nations of the West will have to ask themselves anew just how much scope for progress is left within their present structure of society. It is true that within it they have achieved their relatively high standards of living and won their political liberties. But where do they go from here? Can the Western nations secure full employment as the normal condition of their economy? Can they secure an indefinite continuation of their post-war prosperity? Even if they can, this will allow them merely to maintain a rate of progress which has become manifestly inadequate in comparison with the Soviet rate and inadequate also in relation to the requirements of the present upheaval in science and technology. Are the Western nations socially equipped to absorb and assimilate the now unfolding permanent revolution in technology? Can private enterprise keep pace with state enterprise in technical innovation? These questions are at the heart of the Soviet challenge to the West.

It is one of the Soviet claims that the stimuli for their economic growth are, so to speak, built-in in the public ownership and national planning of industry. Considerations of national, not of private or sectional, profit determine the uninterrupted and vigorous rhythm of economic activity. True, the record of post-war prosperity in the West may suggest that the Western economy too has, on the basis of private enterprise, succeeded in overcoming the anarchy of the old trade cycle; and that it is no longer subject to the spontaneous alternation of boom, slump, and depression. But is it not too early to take this for granted? It should not be forgotten that in the industrial history of the West there were some trade cycles marked by only the mildest of ups and downs. One may find a parallel to the present long-lasting prosperity in the steady development of the German economy in the Bismarck era, when for nearly a quarter of a century, from the early 1870s till the late 1890s, German industry knew no severe slump. This aroused the most optimistic hopes and convinced even many socialists that the Marxist critique of capitalism was out of date. Subsequently, however, the German economy found itself once again in the throes of most violent trade cycles, with very steep ups and downs.

Are Keynesian economic controls (assuming that governments adopt them in time) enough to prevent a similar sequel to the present period of prosperity? The practical evidence of the efficacy of such controls in a situation tending towards a deep slump has yet to be produced. Nor should the view be taken for granted that armament can have or has a continuously stimulating effect on economic activity. Armament may cut both ways: it may stimulate the general demand for goods and investment; but, in certain circumstances, it may restrict them both. Even if this were not so, it would be manifestly dangerous for any nation to rely for its pros-

perity on armament booms. Such a nation would be like
a well fed man who every day takes his large red beef-
steak with a small admixture of poison—he gets all the
proteins and calories he wants and looks healthy and
hale; but he is slowly destroying himself. A prosperity
based on nuclear armaments is deceptive; those who
believe in it implicitly take a defeatist view of the
economic future of the West. I do not think that armament has been so decisive a factor in the post-war
economic upsurge. But I cannot help being struck by a
contrast between Western and Soviet thinking on this
point. While in the West opinion has become as it were
conditioned to treat armament as a stimulus to economic
growth and well-being, in the East opinion is conditioned
to see it as a brake on growth and a drain on prosperity.
While in the West all too often the thought of a slacken-
ing of the arms race conjures up memories of the 1930s
and fears of poverty and unemployment, the Russians,
on the contrary, think confidently of the quickening
tempo of their advance and of the prosperity that would
come within their reach if only they could rid themselves
of the burdens of armament.

This difference shows itself at all levels, in the policies
of governments and the reasonings of the 'man in the
street'. The West has accustomed itself to view the most
unproductive kind of economic activity as a boon in
disguise, while the East recognizes it for what it is—the
irrational waste of immense resources and energies. It
would be ominous for the West to embark upon the new
phase of competitive coexistence in this frame of mind.
The effective Western answer to the Soviet challenge
can lie only in a genuine demonstration of superior
efficiency, that is, of the West's ability to secure,

71

without the 'help' of armament, full employment and continuously rising standards of living, and to secure these while preserving and enlarging its heritage of political freedom. Can Western society, as at present constituted, meet the Soviet challenge in this way?

I have referred to the social and international consequences of the permanent technological revolution now in progress. It may be said that this has to some extent replaced the Marxist prospect of a permanent social revolution. But is the upheaval in technology not preparing another upheaval in social relations? The new technology tends to outgrow our inherited institutions and to render obsolete the frameworks within which we have been accustomed to act, think, and live our lives. It grows above the head of private property. Even in the West atomic power has not been the child of private enterprise. It has been the child of state enterprise. Henceforth nearly every act of the technological upheaval is likely to strengthen the trend towards public ownership and enterprise; the gigantic scale of the new inventions and scientific ventures puts these beyond the resources of private investment. What business concern will undertake to finance the exploration of outer space and face the risks involved in a host of other tremendously expensive pioneering projects which are now maturing in the scientists' minds and laboratories? A state which has the command of the nation's industrial resources is in a far better position to cope with these tasks; and this has been a decisive reason why the Russians have been able partly to overtake the West despite the fact that the West is still so much wealthier. Of their smaller wealth the Russians have been able to make a more concentrated and effective use.

Purposeful and concentrated use of resources is inherent in a nationalized and planned economy. It need not necessarily be achieved at the expense of consumer interests and by a government exercising absolute power, although in Russia it was so achieved in the course of a long period of time. The Russian pattern was part and parcel of 'primitive accumulation', that is of forcible industrialization carried out amid an overall scarcity of resources, and amid the political tensions characteristic of a post-revolutionary period. Since they left that initial phase behind, the Russians have been increasingly able to satisfy consumer needs and at the same time to go on investing on an ever larger scale; and they have started to rid themselves of absolutist government, which far from being the *sine qua non* of the progress of their planned economy, has proved to be an obstacle to it. The more rational and concentrated use of resources in a nationalized economy follows from the organic integration of its elements. This by itself immensely accelerates technological progress. To take one example: no Soviet concern or group of concerns can reserve for itself the advantages of any new invention or innovation and withhold these from others—new methods of production benefit the whole of industry much more quickly than normally happens under private enterprise. No commercial secrecy sets up its own iron or plastic curtains between various sectors of industry (although bureaucratic rigidity may to some extent obstruct the spread of new 'know-how').

Another aspect of the problem, bound to become increasingly important in competitive coexistence, is the relatively greater ability of a nationalized economy to modernize its equipment. Technological revolution necessitates replacement of equipment on an unpre-

73

cedented scale. Other things being equal, the ability of any economy to carry this out in time depends on the strength of the vested interests tied to obsolescent industries. The development of atomic fuel will reduce the importance of coal and petrol. Enormous investments in these industries will become 'prematurely' depreciated. Will those who stand to lose thereby not obstruct the development of atomic fuel in the West? Will the Russians, unimpeded by such obstruction, not jump ahead once again in this all-important field? Significantly, the prospect of the industrial replacement of the old fuels by atomic energy is already being treated by the Russians with far greater urgency than is customary in the West, where the prospect is seen as rather remote.

Automation raises a parallel issue. Some Western industrialists who have had a glimpse of its progress in the Soviet Union maintain that already automation is being carried out there on a scale larger than that attempted in the West. Of course, automation releases great masses of labour. A continuously and rapidly expanding economy can re-deploy and re-employ redundant labour more easily than can be done in a stagnant industry or in one that expands slowly. In addition, the Russians train their labour in a way calculated to endow it with industrial mobility: workers are trained in several skills so as to be able to shift from job to job. How is the West going to handle this problem?

Another and even broader aspect of the Russian challenge is the effort now being made to integrate the economies of the Soviet Union and Eastern Europe and, in the long run, of China also. In their Committee for Economic Mutual Assistance, we know, the Russians have set up the nucleus of an international planning authority. They have launched a number of projects providing for the distribution of manufacturing industries throughout the Soviet Union and Eastern Europe. The purpose is to avoid overlapping in production and to promote specialization and co-ordination, that is planned international division of labour. As I have said before, there are no real tariff walls within the Soviet bloc, and no significant protectionist interests are at work there, although there is, on the other hand, a lot of bureaucratic muddle and there are the political tensions between the Soviet Union and Eastern Europe. However, the absence of strictly economic barriers is a decisive advantage, which enables the members of the Soviet bloc to move economically beyond the nation-state, towards some form of international society.

How will the West respond to this challenge? Can it overcome its economic nationalisms, overrule its protectionist interests, sweep away its tariff barriers, and integrate its economies? Can the great industrial concerns of North America combine with those of Western Europe and jointly initiate and plan an international division of labour? At the moment Western Europe is split into a Common Market and a Free Trade Area; and each of these views uneasily the competitive potentialities of the United States. The Soviet-sponsored Common Market has greater unity: the objective of policy there is to integrate not merely trading areas but industries. It should be repeated that if the Soviet plan succeeds, then this communist Common Market and integrated economy will form an entity which, in the last quarter of this century, may be four or five times as large as the North American market and twice as large as a combined North American and Western European market would be. If only to hold its ground the West will need a great deal of further economic expansion and much impetus in overcoming national separatisms in its midst.

I should like to reconsider for a moment the repercussions in the under-developed countries. People there see what Russia, herself an under-developed nation until recently, has achieved on the basis of public ownership and planning; and now they watch China repeating the Soviet performance in easier circumstances, with less violence, and perhaps more successfully. It is only natural that they should ponder whether they themselves should not follow in Russia's and China's footsteps. They may not be aware of the price in suffering and oppression the Russians have paid for their ascendancy. But even if they are aware of it, they have ground for hope that they themselves would not need to pay in full the price that Russia as the pioneer in socialization and planning had to pay. And to people without the tradition of bourgeois democracy, the price may not seem at all prohibitive.

Relations between India and China (and the rest of the Soviet bloc) are crucial in this context. Here there is a gigantic focus for all the dilemmas of competitive co-existence. Already China has been much quicker than India in the economic uptake. Indian economists point out that the increase in India's agricultural production has been so slow compared with the growth of population that in only a few years from now tens of millions of men and women in India may be condemned to starvation if nothing drastic is at once undertaken to change the outlook; and nothing drastic, it appears, is being undertaken. Meantime the Chinese are greatly increasing their food output—they are said to grow more rice than is produced in the rest of the world, and to distribute it to their workers virtually free of charge. The contrast could not be more striking; and it would become most dramatic if indeed many millions of Indians were to be threatened with famine and China's rice surplus were to secure their survival. This would be a signal development in the struggle between communism and anti-communism in Asia. The effect of China's industrialization will similarly show itself in the coming decade. China owes her advantages to the transformation of her social order and to Soviet help. Can the West help the under-developed countries in a way as effective as that in which the Soviet Union has aided China? Can any foreign assistance be as effective in an under-developed country which maintains its archaic social structure (landlordism and the caste system) intact?

The Soviet Union has, as a rule, been assisting China and other under-developed countries not with consumer goods but with industrial equipment and technical knowledge. Soviet experts train technicians and workers in China and other countries of Asia; and vast numbers of technicians and workers from those countries are studying in Soviet universities and technological colleges and learning industrial skills in Soviet factories. This is the cheapest and the most effective assistance: it costs far less than does American aid in consumer goods; and it helps the under-developed nations to help themselves. The effect of American assistance is largely ephemeral, and this is why, to their pained surprise, it earns the Americans so little gratitude. The results of Soviet assistance are lasting; and those who receive it have the sense of being raised up from backwardness and dependence. The Russians say: 'We can do all this because we are not afraid of foreign competition; we do not tremble for our markets; and we are not afraid of sharing industrial know-how. Western capitalists cannot afford to do this.' Here is another challenge which the West has to meet.

I have dwelt until now on the economic issues of competitive coexistence. These have so far been foremost in the Western mind. Much though Western statesmen, politicians, and commentators may despise dialectical materialism (or what passes for it), they are, I am afraid, inclined to approach competitive coexistence in a narrowly materialistic spirit. Yet it cannot be repeated often enough that the chief issue is not who will outproduce whom and when, or even who will eventually have the higher standards of living, important though all this is. Ultimately the challenge is a spiritual one. Even now the fields in which the West finds it most difficult to match the Soviet advance are those of social policy and education. The Russians are completing their transition to the 35–40-hour week in industry (the 35-hour week has been introduced in mining and other dangerous or difficult occupations); and they plan a further reduction to 30–35 hours between 1964 and 1968. Western Europe is working long hours. Even in England only a few trade unions are just beginning to demand a 40-hour week. The workers often compensate for the long hours by economizing their energy and working slowly and sluggishly. Western European industry is in no mood to introduce (or re-introduce) the 40-hour week. When the Russians do go over to 30–35 hours, will even North American industry be inclined to emulate this example? Yet the working classes of the West will certainly grow increasingly aware of the disadvantage under which they will be placed. Here is the greatest challenge in social policy with which the West is going to be confronted.

As to education, we know that the Russians train many more engineers and technicians than does any Western country, including the United States. They have developed a unique system of extramural adult education. And above all, their social and educational policies are closely interlinked. While social policy aims at the continuous shortening of working hours and at lightening the burdens of productive work, educational policy envisages an unprecedented spread and improvement of educational facilities. It is this that gives social and cultural sense to the shortening of hours in industry. The worker, as he leaves his factory after a shorter day, is being enabled to make civilized use of his leisure. He does not fall a prey to commercialized entertainment and to the stultifying vulgarities of a sensational press and television. True, his leisure is all too often spoilt by assaults of dogmatic propaganda. It used to be said of the English Puritans that they made people eat bread with religion, and people could not stand it. Stalinism has made the Russians eat bread with ideology. Under Khrushchev they have more bread and less ideology, but they are still being stuffed with a lot of stodgy dogma. Indigestible as this is, it has at least the redeeming feature that it does not lower in the working man the level of his human interests as much as our commercialized 'mass media' do. Despite all their faults the Russian 'mass media' tend to instruct minds rather than to stunt them; they try at least to develop in people a sense of social community and solidarity; and sometimes they do it on a level of seriousness which should be the envy of the West. Whatever may be said in criticism of the

Soviet 'way of life', it does not produce the Lonely Crowd.

Nor should we underrate the appeal that the vision of future achievement has on the mass of the people. It gives them what may be described as an anti-Orwell image of 1984. The Russians are encouraged to expect that by that time they may obtain a working day of not more than four or even three hours. Is this a wild dream? I do not think so. Technological advance should allow the reduction of the working day even to three or two hours before the end of this century. About a hundred years ago the idea of a six- or seven-hour day would have seemed wild to our ancestors; yet labour-saving machinery has made it possible to reduce the working day by half and to multiply the wealth of the industrial nations. In all probability, the next forty years will bring progress in labour-saving far greater than that achieved in the last hundred years—and with it the possibility of a reduction of the present working day by at least one half. With only two to three hours' work in an automated industry man would indeed cease to 'eat his bread in the sweat of his brow'; and if the educational system expands as the 'socially necessary' productive labour shrinks, then equal opportunity for all *will* become a reality.

The time of universal academic education may not be so very far off—it may perhaps come even before the end of this century. Again, we should not shrug this off as a pipe dream: did not the idea of universal secondary education seem 'impossible' even at the beginning of this century?

With the work for his livelihood occupying only a small part of his active life, man will be able to spend the rest of his time pursuing intellectual and aesthetic interests, studying, enjoying art, exploring the universe, engaging in sport, and so on. The division of society into the toilers and the leisured classes would then vanish; and with it could disappear the divorce and the gulf between intellectual work and manual labour. The former would cease to be the privilege of a minority, the latter—a dire necessity and a curse for the mass of mankind.

Of course, this is no new ideal. But hitherto ideal and reality have been poles apart; and no path could be seen leading to Utopia. Now at last, the Russians think, technological progress and social and educational developments do begin to throw a solid bridge between the realities of today and the vision of the future.

This is an inspiring vista, and no pooh-poohing it will diminish its attraction. Has the West something better, more realistic, or more inspiring to offer? This is the greatest single question of competitive coexistence.

Of course, there is freedom, political freedom, in the West; and this is absent from the Soviet Union and the communist-ruled countries. The moral importance of this contrast can hardly be overrated. But I do not think that the contrast will last indefinitely. The Russians have already discovered that they need freedom, if only to be socially efficient. In the years to come they will be discovering that the doses of freedom their rulers grant them are too small and meagre. They will clamour for more and, I think, the rulers will have to meet the demand. As I see it, the coming decade will bring a gradual, or not so gradual, enlargement of civil liberty, although there will also be temporary setbacks and there may occur dramatic clashes between the rulers and the ruled.

These prospects will affect competitive coexistence.

Hitherto the West has won many a moral and political battle against Russia because Russia was a tyranny and the goddess of freedom fought on the Western side. In the West were also the big industrial battalions. Now Russia is forming and marshalling her big industrial battalions; and the new Soviet generation longs to see the goddess of freedom in its camp; and it may yet tempt her over there. And then the moral advantage the West has so far enjoyed may dwindle.

There are various ways in which the West can face this multiple challenge. It may react with fear and panic; or it may respond with courage and enterprise. It may cling to outdated institutions and social forms; or it may embark upon a bold search for new modes of organization and upon radical changes in the framework of society. The West still has tremendous assets. It has an industrial start over the Soviet bloc: after all, it is still the Soviet aspiration to catch up with the United States. The advantage of political freedom, though far from intact, is still with the West. The West is richer in cultural tradition—its cultural heritage is older and more varied than Russia's. With such assets, if only it does not dissipate them, if only it puts them to the proper use, and if it guards against panicky as well as wishful thinking, the West should have nothing to fear and should be well able to hold its ground. If only the West learns to face the future instead of clinging to the past, the challenge will hold no threat to it; and—who knows?—competitive coexistence may yet change from the bitter competition it is into co-operative emulation. This certainly is the only hope. The alternative may be mutual extermination.

I would like to conclude my remarks with the words

which the Dafoe Foundation, as whose guest I have had the honour to speak here, uses as the text of its activities, words written by J. W. Dafoe, the great Canadian Editor:

I am convinced [he wrote], it is the faith by which I live, that all these difficulties arise from conditions that are temporary, and that we are moving irresistibly by the discoveries of science, by the ingenuity of man, by the necessities of our life, to the condition of a world community of peace in which there will be harmonious co-operation between great nations and small nations.

These words evoke a melancholy reflection. Dafoe wrote them in the year 1930; nine years later what was to have been 'a world community of peace' was engulfed in the Second World War. Yet I think that Dafoe's words have lost nothing of their truth—their message has become even more urgent. The Second World War was the last occasion when the Great Powers could still clash in arms without annihilating themselves and mankind. We dare not afford a repetition; we dare not allow, in this nuclear age, the hope expressed by Dafoe to be frustrated once more. We must see to it that the difficulties with which we are confronted do indeed prove temporary; and that the 'discoveries of science, the ingenuity of man, and the necessities of our life' do indeed 'lead us to a condition of a world community of peace'. Dafoe said: 'it is the faith by which I live'. We must know that only if we *act* on that faith shall we live at all.

INDEX